DR. JOE: A LIFETIME OF SERVICE

A Biography of Joseph Schmiedicke

EDGEWOOD COLLEGE

Mary Ellen Gevelinger, O.P.

AuthorHouse™
1663 Liberty Drive
Bloomington, IN 47403
www.authorhouse.com
Phone: 1-800-839-8640

© 2009 Mary Ellen Gevelinger, O.P.. All rights reserved.

No part of this book may be reproduced, stored in a retrieval system, or transmitted by any means without the written permission of the author.

First published by AuthorHouse 5/12/2009

ISBN: 978-1-4389-7961-8 (sc)
ISBN: 978-1-4389-7962-5 (hc)

Printed in the United States of America
Bloomington, Indiana

This book is printed on acid-free paper.

CONTENTS

Forward vii

Introduction xi

Part I: Family of Origin 1

    1. Parents and Maternal Grandparents 3
    2. Paternal Grandparents and Family Business 7
    3. Childhood Memories 12
    4. Influence of World Events 17
    5. My Siblings: The oldest four Jerry and Tom, Mary and Linda 20
    6. My Siblings: The Younger Six Sue Ann, Bill, and Donna, Rita, Paul and Ruth 28
    7. Influence of Church 38
    8. Seminary Life at St. Joseph's High School and Junior College 43
    9. Theological College at Catholic University of America 53
    10. Marquette University 61

Family Photos 67

Part II: Family of Choice: Marriage and Children 71

    11. David Schmiedicke and Cherie Schmiedicke, his Wife 75
    12. Mary Schmiedicke Hong 81
    13. Lisa Schmiedicke Mure 84
    14. Megan Schmiedicke Fox 87
    15. Our Dad, Joe 89

    16. Our Schmiedicke Grandparents 102
    17. Our Mother, Marian 106
    18. Marsha Callahan 115
    19. Joe's Legacy—in David's Words..................... 119

Family Photos 121

Part III: Edgewood Family 1963-2009 127

    20. Edgewood College 129
    21. Sinsinawa Dominican Sponsorship................. 134
    22. Dr. Joe, Gourmet Chef.................................... 138
    23. Truth... 142
    24. Compassion 148
    25. Justice 152
    26. Community 155
    27. Partnership.. 159
    28. Leadership... 163
    29. Early Days at Edgewood: Mentors and
         Friends 167
    30. Awards, Honors and Tributes 174

Notes 181

Acknowledgements 183

FORWARD

The author of this book, Dr. Mary Ellen Gevelinger, O.P., and the subject of this book, Dr. Joe Schmiedicke, are two people with whom I have had the great pleasure to be counted as a colleague and a friend. Dr. Joe has been a stalwart at Edgewood College for 46 years. He has taken on or advised nearly every leadership position imaginable. He has been a catalyst for important, nay crucial, growth of the college. One cannot think of the Edgewood College Education Department, now the School of Education, without thinking of Dr. Joe. Within this book one will see his unbending faith in the importance of education and in God, evident in the durable and resilient ethical and moral foundation that he found in the Catholic Church and the Dominican traditions within that church. They are the traditions and values that formed the basis of his servant leadership approach to his management and ministry of the preparation of future educators. His tireless toiling for the future of not only the profession of education, but for the safe future of the world, are evident in the pages of this text, as told by the many around him who shared his life and vision. Also evident in these pages is a story of how four or five generations of a devout and dedicated family live, laugh, and cry together. The bonds formed by family provide an example of the strength needed by all of us to survive, if not physically, at least morally and ethically.

Cor ad cor loquitor, heart speaks to heart, has been the cornerstone of Dr. Joe's professional life. It is the basic tenet of the Dominican values that shape his work at Edgewood College. Schooled in the classical languages and a Latin teacher in his youth, Dr. Joe epitomizes the all-too-rare Renaissance man today. Beginning with his youth in the family construction trade Dr. Joe has been a builder throughout his career. He helped Edgewood build the professional school of education into, first, a great foundational undergraduate experience for students, he then constructed the second floor of a Master's Degree, and most recently the third floor of a leadership doctoral program. He built with words that which his family built with wood.

In addition to expanding the horizon of the college with programs and degrees, Dr. Joe was instrumental in strengthening the internal mechanisms as well. Recruiting faculty and students, organizing conferences and conventions, directing the summer school, inviting alumnae to participate in the growth and development of college programs, pushing the issue of technology integration in the curriculum, finding resources to support growth, advocating for faculty, advising Presidents and Trustees, and finding time for a student to sit in his office and muse were all part of a day's work for Dr. Joe. He will be missed!

This Forward would not be complete without a special note of appreciation to Sister Mary Ellen for accepting the daunting task of compiling and writing this book. What a job! She has skillfully provided a picture of a career professional and pedagogue, Dr. Joe, as the nucleus of this work, surrounded by the orbits of his family, colleagues, and friends; all of this of this while maintaining a more than full-time position of Director of Research for the Education Doctoral Program at Edgewood. Congratulations and thank you, Mary Ellen, on a job well done!

Peter Burke

Director, Doctoral Program at Edgewood College

3/10/09

INTRODUCTION

"a wise young man from the East bearing gifts for us all"
Juventus sapiens ab oriente venit, portans dona pro omnes....

St. Dominic Villa

Sinsinawa, Wisconsin

December 8, 2008

Dear Dr. Joe,

    What a joy it has been to read the good things about you, and remember many more with gratitude, beginning with your arrival from Michigan, a wise young man from the East bearing gifts for us all. Thank you for the model you offered us as a teacher of teachers and Christian gentleman.

    Come to see your friends at Sinsinawa in visiting weather. God bless you!

(signed)

Sister Mary Nona McGreal, OP [1]

With prescient insight, Sister Mary Nona McGreal, in her 90's, and residing at St. Dominic Villa, Sinsinawa, at this writing, recalls her hiring of young Joseph Schmiedicke for Edgewood College, *as "a wise young man from the East bearing gifts for us all."* Sister Mary Nona McGreal, OP, was the first named President of Edgewood College and served the College from 1950-1968. As there were not enough Dominican Sisters of Sinsinawa available and academically prepared to serve as college faculty, Sister Nona was seeking lay faculty to meet the needs of the growing college programs. One of her fortuitous hires, in 1963, was the young Mr. Schmiedicke, a recently minted M.Ed. from Marquette University in Milwaukee, Wisconsin. This is his life story.

What influences, circumstances, world and family events came together to bring this man to Edgewood College in the early 1960's? The circuitous and interesting story demands to be told from the beginning. It has been said that "where you grow up has its tendrils in you." For Joe Schmiedicke, those tendrils lead directly back to his home and family. The early setting for the Schmiedicke family is Grand Rapids, Michigan, with a population of 137,634 in 1920, according to census records from the US Census Bureau. [2]

Grand Rapids, on the banks of the Grand River, is approximately 30 miles east of Lake Michigan, and the county seat of Kent County. The city was a significant railroad connection during the late 1800's, and boasted being a furniture manufacturer and lumbering center. This lumber and railroad designation would have an influence on the Schmiedicke family and their business in the 20th Century. The Grand River was the main mode of transportation for floating logs from the forests of the north into the factories of Grand Rapids. Workers for the large furniture factories expanding in the city came from the immigrant populations arriving from Germany, Ireland, Sweden, Poland and Italy. The arrival of large numbers of immigrants fostered the creation of ethnic neighborhoods, complete with grocery stores, bakeries, along with schools and churches to serve the needs of the residents.

By the beginning of the 20th century, the city boasted more than 50 furniture factories involved in furniture manufacturing and related industries, such as sawmills, paint and varnish companies, and manufacturers of woodworking machinery. Construction businesses for commercial and residential buildings abounded. These businesses flourished until the late 1920's. With the arrival of the Great Depression, at least half of the furniture and related factories closed. Businesses that could adapt to changing needs in changing times remained in the Grand Rapids community.[3] The city has continued to grow, and in 2007 boasted a population of 193,627, as the second largest city in Michigan, according to the US Census Bureau website.[4]

The journey of that *young man from the East*, Joseph Schmiedicke, began in Grand Rapids, Michigan, and is told in the following chapters. In Part I, Dr. Joe tells the story in his own words. In Part II, adult children David, Mary, Lisa and Megan, wife Marsha, and daughter-in-law Cherie lend their voices to the tale. Part III relies primarily on the recordings and written tributes from colleagues, friends, and alumnae of Edgewood College.

I

FAMILY OF ORIGIN

1

PARENTS AND MATERNAL GRANDPARENTS

Bona Fortuna **Good Fortune**

"Well, I was born in Grand Rapids, Michigan, on January 31, 1938. My mother, Madeline T. Lybarger, and father, Edward E. Schmiedicke, met each other at what was called the Sunshine Sanitarium of Kent County in Michigan. My father was a patient and my mother was a nurse. There was in my father's family the tuberculosis tradition, my grandfather had it and my father had it and I suspect that if I were living back in those days, I probably would have had it but due to the good fortune of medicine that has developed over time I do not have it.

"My place in the family is first child. I'm the oldest of eleven children. At the time my parents were living with my paternal grandparents, Margaret Fox Schmiedicke and Ernest Schmiedicke; my great grandmother, Rosa, was also a member of the family. So there was an extended family living together, a couple of my uncles and aunts…it was, I can't say a conscious awareness on my part at the time, but I do believe that helped set some of the frameworks for the future. We lived pretty much together for about five years at 304 Straight Avenue, in Grand Rapids. It was about 1943 that my parents bought a home nearby, actually just two blocks away, at 200 Straight Avenue. Those two homes are still owned by the family.

"On the maternal side of the family, my mother, Madeline Therese Lybarger, was one of six children, all girls. Her father, Burdett, preferred to be known as B.A. He was the pharmacist in the town of Hastings, Michigan, about 30 miles south of Grand Rapids, where I was born. My grandfather was educated at Ferris State University in Michigan, and I think today we'd probably call him a homeopathic pharmacist because he had kind of a mix of some of the old herbal approaches to treatment. I still to this day remember the smells of the pharmacy…the balsam and the various types of herbs, and once in a while if I smell it I will think of that. B.A. Lybarger, he always went by B. A. because he did not like his names of Burdett Albert. Occasionally my grandmother, Genevieve Breuten Lybarger, would call him **Burdett a**nd we knew something was up. But the people and his customers and so on called him Dr. B.A. because he provided so much advice to people on how to deal with their health concerns, particularly what we would call today the homeopathic approaches to healing.

"The pharmacy influence is interesting. My grandfather had a pharmacy in downtown Hastings, Michigan. It was in one of these old buildings that had probably twenty foot ceilings. He had two floors, first floor, second floor and a set of stairs that must have gone up forever. You'd walk up those stairs and it would take you five minutes to get up to the top. And upstairs was where he stored all of his things. Now, you know drugstores today have a variety of inventory and amazingly enough, so did he. He sold paint. He sold school supplies. I still remember the Car Ferry books, spiral Car Ferry books. He also of course was the pharmacist and one full wall on the west side of his building was filled with carefully constructed wooden drawers. We'd get lessons from Grandfather B.A. on which drawers you could touch and which ones you couldn't. And it was always tempting to get into the drawers that we couldn't. The warnings, of course, were based on some of the likely downside risks of some of the plants and things that he had.

"He, at one point was saying, 'You know you're going to have to make some life decisions about what you're doing some day and you tell your mother and father that you want to be a pharmacist and you will come down here and you'll work with me and I will see that eventually you will take over my business.' That was his expressed dream for me.

"Unfortunately, his dream was never realized, largely because I wasn't interested in all the plants, quite frankly. And I'm not sure why, but it was later, maybe expressed in one of the high school classes that I took in chemistry. I had an instructor that was named Mr. Belardo. I was in the seminary at this time. And Mr. Belardo was our instructor for two years of chemistry and I don't know why but I would go up to Mr. Belardo and say things like, 'Mr. Belardo where are the Bunsen burners?' And he would say, 'Mr. Schmiedicke, the Bunsen burners are, as I told you, in the box marked *Bunsen burners*.' And I would say something to the effect, 'You know, my grandfather used to tell me about these boxes and told me to keep my hands off 'em so I was never quite interested in the boxes that the Bunsen burners were in,' but…. And then I would ask, 'Well can we light the Bunsen burners?' 'No, not until I give you instructions.' Well, I said, it sounds like my grandfather again. At any rate, the sciences as science never really interested me that much until I got to Catholic University and then, you know, I had gone too far in life to start over. But we had some interesting teachers at Catholic University so I did well in science, but I just wasn't interested back when Grandfather would like me to have been a pharmacist.

2

PATERNAL GRANDPARENTS AND FAMILY BUSINESS

Cura nihil aliud nisi ut valeas.

Pay attention to nothing except that you do well. Cicero

"My paternal grandfather, Ernest, was from the construction industry, actually was a cabinet maker originally and part of the woodworking industry. Grand Rapids, as you may know, was a major furniture site during the 19th century. It's what originally brought my great grandfather, I am told, from Manitowoc, Wisconsin, to Grand Rapids, Michigan. He was a German Evangelical Lutheran and married my grandmother, a Catholic, Rosa Sailor. And Rosa Schmiedicke was my great grandmother who was living with us at the house in Grand Rapids at the time that I was born. My father was one of five children, three boys and two girls. One of his sisters had died at birth, Minnie Schmiedicke.

"In both of the situations, the family being very influential in my development, I have spent a lot of time in both the pharmacy and in construction. Let me tell just a couple of stories. When I was about five years old my father and his father, my grandfather, formed a corporation called Woodworking Industries, Inc. of Grand Rapids, MI. They did that in order to respond to a RFP, (request for proposal), I think we'd call it today, with the federal government to build prefabricated barracks for World War II. They had a large factory building where they did all of their work in making the units that were eventually assembled and sent from Grand Rapids to San Francisco and then out to the Pacific front. They built what were called Tropical Barracks for the armed services.

"These barracks would be erected out in the South Pacific theatre of the war. They would work basically five and a half days of the week. On Saturday mornings they would work approximately from eight o'clock until noon, and I would go along with them on Saturday mornings for half a day about maybe twice a month. I can still remember a lot of the conditions of that factory which were exciting to a five-year-old because I got to ride on dollies that ran on train tracks through the factory. I got to ride on this big freight elevator with a wooden gate, I got to go onto the roof with my grandfather at noon and take down the American flag and what was called the Army Navy E Flag and fold them up. And, I got to see the operation from the ground up.

"Just recently, one of my brothers in Michigan found a box that has some of the records of that business, Woodworking Industries, Inc., and we were going through it together. There were a few pictures in there, my grandfather's in one of them and a handwritten record by Grandpa Ernie as we call him, all of the incoming lumber and all of the outgoing units. And as you look down the list of things you see like PRR, Pennsylvania RR, you see CNW, Chicago Northwestern, and there must be at least a dozen train lines that came in and out of there. And, it's astounding, the amount of lumber, the hundreds of thousands of board feet of lumber that they recorded. Even to the detail of things like hemlock, air-dried hemlock, green hemlock, and then as we were looking at it I thought that this brings back my memory of my grandfather's admonition to many of us, it was, 'Now if you're going to do anything in lumber in your house, never use green lumber because it shrinks, and the walls will start to crack, or the building will start to get weak.'

"This construction company was built right on the railroad. As a matter of fact it was about six blocks from the major train yard in Grand Rapids and just west of the Grand River which runs through the center of town. There was a side track that ran over to this building, and the track actually just continued down into the factory because they could drive through two ends of the building, and bring in the large box cars that delivered the board lumber and where they loaded them, and they went out with the units ready to be assembled out in the South Pacific.

"This is a great snapshot of life at that point and how people were creative and responding. They had many different kinds of orientations to their businesses over time. It was always related to construction in some way or another. Their business that was unrelated to the war effort was the E.J. Schmiedicke and Sons, and that was their general construction company.

"And, I received many admonitions from my grandfather and learned many lessons from working with them in that business. I actually started with them in a formal way at about the age of eleven. And there were times that I'd be working with them at let's say the construction of the family home or something like that, during summers or vacation time. 'It's time to backfill, Joe, the holes around the foundation,' my grandfather would say. 'Oh, I'm not sure I want to shovel dirt today,' I'd respond. 'Everybody has to shovel dirt at some time in their life.'

"I don't even remember all the conditions, but there was a time when I said something to my grandfather to the effect of… Well you know, I have a real important influence on this business and he said, 'Well, I'll tell you what, Joe, if you think that's true, you go get a bucket of water and bring the bucket of water over here.' So I went and got a bucket of water and brought it over. He said, 'Now put your hands in there and slosh around in that bucket.' And then he says, 'Go over there and wipe off your hands and come back in about ten minutes.' And I did. And he says, 'Well look what's happenin' to the water as a result of your sloshing your hands around.' And it was as peaceful and calm as could be. He said, 'That's about how much influence you have.'

"There was a lot of wisdom that was being shared. And, you know, it was responsive to a situation immediately. It wasn't like a kind of synthetic or artificial teaching, but it was taught…It was homegrown wisdom.

3

CHILDHOOD MEMORIES

Historia est vitae magistra. **History is the tutor of life.**

"As for childhood memories, one thing that pops out immediately, about the age of five or six, probably five, I had just received a new bike and I was riding my bike around the block. I got within about half a block of home and I fell off my bike, and I could not get up. My sister, Mary, saw me and she ran in the house to get my mother. Before my mother could come out of the house, the only black man in the neighborhood came by and picked me up and carried me. His name was John Phillips. He was the only black person that I think I ever knew in my life, up to that point, and I just could not believe he would stop and pick me up. It was just out of my experience. He was a mailman and had been discharged from the army maybe about a year or a year and a half before that. They lived about a block and a half from us. We knew where they were, but we didn't know them in any significant way. And on the way home, carrying me home he was saying, 'You know you probably hurt, but you'll be all right.' And he took me up to the front porch of the house and gave me to my mother. She said, 'Are you all right?' And I said, 'Yes, can I have some cookies?' Well, of course, I went to the hospital, and I had the cast on my foot for awhile.

"I broke my leg. At that time my father and my grandfather had been asked to do a major construction job for my uncle and aunt in Hastings, Michigan, and they decided that it would be best for them and everybody, I guess, to move to my grandfather's cottage just outside Hastings on Wall Lake.

"But…what to do with Joe because he has this broken leg. So Joe went to live with his grandparents, and my grandmother, Margaret, took care of me for quite a bit of time. My parents would return to Grand Rapids on weekends. I could not imagine how much I missed them, …but, Grandma did a good job. And pretty soon it was time for the cast to come off. And…Grandma… Grandma was an interesting person. Grandma did all the books for the business. Grandma also took good care of herself: she went to the salon every week, she went to bridge every week, she went to movies. And I got introduced to a lot of movies. Some I didn't want to see. But, it was interesting that she took very good care of me, and she said, 'Now Joe, you haven't been able to run much because of the broken leg in the cast. What would you like to do?' And I said, 'I'd like to see Mom and Dad out at the cottage.' 'Well, that's a good idea.' So she got a friend of hers, because everybody was gone down to the cottage. She got a friend of hers to come over one afternoon…it was one of her bridge colleagues…and her name I cannot remember…they lived up on the northwest side of town. At any rate, she came over with her car and Grandma and her friend took me out to the cottage. And, I got a chance to see Mom and Dad and I actually stayed overnight. And then…it was like a Thursday or a Friday and I stayed until the weekend and I went back with them. That's one of the experiences that stands out and it has so many pieces to it. I return to it quite often…it's just amazing.

"And…there's a subset of the telephone in that. The telephone is interesting. My father did not believe in telephones. There was not a phone in my house until I had left home. I was 25 before there was a phone in that house. The phone was in the house because Linda felt it was time that the parents could be contacted by phone. What? How do you run a business without a phone? Well, you run a business without a phone because you live two blocks from Grandma's and Grandma runs all the books and takes all the messages and has the phone…Glendale 4-96-98. It resulted in an interesting communication system. Grandma would come down to the house every once in a while and say, 'Well, Ed, Bob Johnson wants you to call him because his cottage needs a new roof.' And dad would say, 'Okay, I'll do that. As a matter of fact, I'll send a postcard tomorrow.' The interesting thing about this is that Bob Johnson preferred to communicate by a postcard. He didn't like to make phone calls either. He'd call my grandma and he'd say, 'You know, go down there and tell Ed that I want a postcard from him tomorrow.' And so, Bob

Johnson would do all of his communication by postcard and set up the schedule and do all the business that way.

"Or...on occasion, Grandma would say, 'Whoever...wants you to come over and measure some things and give them an estimate on...' And Dad would say, 'Okay, I'll write that up for you, Ma, and I'll get that back to you tomorrow.' And he would write up...everything he wrote was in the script of the architect. It's very formed. His father wrote the same way...clear as could be. My handwriting is terrible but his draftsmen training, I think, came out. And the communications that he wrote were to the point and very, very clear in terms of handwriting. It was just amazing.

"My father also was very interested in stamp collecting, and he maintained an international communication, handwritten to people all over the world that rose out of his tuberculosis. He became fascinated with the TB seals and that led him further into stamps. So as an avocation during his free time, whenever that was, he would write one or two page letters, and they'd all be in that architectural script. I have twenty-two letters of communication that he maintained with places, and I think that led me to some understanding of the world, that there was a world out there. Denmark, Cuba, etc.

"He kept all those communications, and then I was able to organize them. I have samples and actual stamps and seals and things like that from those various correspondences that he maintained with people. It's interesting because I don't think I appreciated this when I was a kid growing up, but I knew it was happening, and I would see the mail come in from different parts of the world. It's a fascinating collection because it reveals a kind of interest worldwide in this disease. And he writes some of his experiences into that from his sanitarium experience and writes some of his interest into it about what can be done by the sale of seals to support medical research, so to speak.

"It wasn't organized, but just as he left it. He had it in brown envelopes--almost always from the original writer of the letter. The fascinating thing about that is you have all the basic materials. As a matter of fact, when I first saw it I thought, 'oh, what am I getting myself into?' But it has been very, very interesting. As a matter of fact, I haven't finished it yet. That always fascinated me, but what really fascinated me was two years after he died, the family asked me to go through the collection and organize it. I've prepared about 20 three-ring binders, reflecting an international correspondence, representing between 50 and 60 cities, worldwide. The family is discussing whether to donate it to a Museum such as Winterthur, the DuPont Estate in Delaware, a Museum of American Furniture and Ephemera. Occasionally, I make a kind of report to the family and it's usually at the summer reunion that we have. We skipped last year because there were a couple of people who had very serious cancer problems. I think next year we'll have another one.

4

INFLUENCE OF WORLD EVENTS

Dictum sapient sat est. **A word to the wise is sufficient.**

"World events impacted our family and our business in more ways than I realized as I was growing up. I've alluded to the construction business and its relationship to the war. At the age of 5 or 6, my father was called up for the draft. That was very traumatic for him. He didn't want to go and have his physical exam in Detroit. My mother and I took him to the train station to make his trip to Detroit. I can remember her clearly telling him he wouldn't be drafted because he had had tuberculosis. And as a matter of fact, that's what happened.

Mary Ellen Gevelinger, O.P.

"I also remember very distinctly we would have blackouts in the evening. There would be a block warden that would come around from house to house, and if they saw any light they would stop. And one night he stopped at our house because he could see a glow. In the living room, the radio was on, and the light on the radio could be seen outside. We had to turn the radio off. We were listening about a possible invasion on the West coast of the United States.

"For my grandchildren who may be reading this, I'll describe a blackout. A siren would go off in the town. Everyone was to go into their homes or a protective facility, like a church, and all lights had to be turned off. Everyone would have to stay in until an *all clear* signal was given. These were practices for the occasion that might occur when a bomber might come and drop explosives on the town. It was shortly after the invasion of the Japanese in Pearl Harbor, so if an invasion would occur on the west coast, those bombs would originate from the Japanese. War was the world that shaped our early years.

"The other thing that I remember from that time was that my uncle Bob, whom I adored, was called up and drafted. He left for service. My grandmother had a little flag with a star that she hung in the window, indicating that someone had been drafted into the military. She displayed that very proudly in the living room.

"Another clearly distinctive memory was VE Day, in 1945. Everyone went downtown, hundreds of people showed up, horns went off, everyone was cheering. That was to celebrate the Victory over Europe.

"I also remember the impact of President Roosevelt who was providing a way of coming out of the depression, and the social fabric was being rebuilt. I remember a lot of conversation. I remember my father lobbying my grandfather to get involved in Social Security. It was kind of the safety net. At the end, my father and his mother prevailed, and grandpa had to come along. They had agreed that they would put the family business supporting Social Security.

"My real consciousness of federal, political and governmental realities doesn't really occur until I entered Catholic University, and it was a very famous person, a congressman, Gerald Ford, from Grand Rapids, Michigan. When I went to Catholic University, it was announced in the **Grand Rapids Catholic Herald,** that I was chosen for the Basselin Scholarship. He wrote a letter congratulating me and inviting me to come to his office. He would take me around, and we'd have lunch. It was then that the role of government and its impact became a bit more intensive in my understanding.

5

MY SIBLINGS: THE OLDEST FOUR: JERRY AND TOM, MARY AND LINDA

Domus dulcis domus **Home sweet home**

"Because of the size of the family and because of the situation of my education after high school, the siblings that I'm closest to are probably the first four after me. So that's Jerry and Tom, and Mary and Linda. I know them best, they know me best and we have a long-standing relationship. The circumstance that I experienced in leading me to the seminary led my brother Jerry, who's my immediate sibling in birth order, to the seminary also. He was there about one year and said, 'This is not for me!' So he left. But I think he too was influenced by the appreciation of education and higher education in our family. He was the first of the siblings to encounter Dominican education because he went to Aquinas College in Grand Rapids. It was through him that I began to be involved in some of the education at Aquinas.

"I have a long story about that but there were some other things that happened in his life that were, you know, (Sister Nona would call them providential). We used to travel on Thanksgiving Day from Grand Rapids to B.A.'s house (my maternal grandfather) in Hastings for Thanksgiving dinner. On one occasion coming back, I was a student at St. Joseph's Seminary at the time and Jerry was at Catholic Central High School at the time, we had just left Hastings on our return trip to Grand Rapids, about 30 miles. It was snowing very heavily. We had just left Hastings, probably we were four miles out of Hastings, and had just started up a hill and my father said, 'We are going to be in an accident.' A car was coming down the hill and could not stop. Our car was filled with about six children at the time and two adults. My brother was sitting in the front seat between my father and myself, and we were struck. My father had gone off the right side of the road as far as he could, and then there was a barrier because we were going up a hill. And we were hit head-on; so that was a major accident.

"It happened that I had a camera in the car at the time. We took pictures of it all. I started my techie interests early. That's the result of the influence of my Grandfather B.A. Lybarger. He collected cameras and took a lot of pictures himself and the camera that I had was a gift from him when I went into the seminary. At any rate, I took pictures of the accident.

"As a result of the accident, there were three of us that ended up in the hospital overnight, but my brother, Jerry, was in for about two or three days, because the front of his legs had become smashed for all practical purposes. Because we had the pictures of the accident and how it happened, the attorneys for the case were able to get Jerry's injuries and everything covered by their settlement. They also received for him a settlement that was designed to help him maintain his educational status. And because of that, and with the influence of one of the priests at St. James, he eventually decided to go to Black Rock College in Dublin, Ireland, for one year to finish out his high school work. That was probably eye-opening both for him and for me because he would write pretty regularly from Black Rock about what he was doing, what was happening.

" Jerry has his master's degree from Michigan State University. Jerry is also an operator and I think probably the best example of that is when he left high school, he went to the seminary. He lasted a year and when he left, his first employment opportunity was as a shoe salesman, and he was one of the best in Grand Rapids. He quickly got out of that as he finished his education, but it was a way to keep busy, I guess. He eventually became the director of the social welfare agencies for the State of Michigan, for a four county area in central Michigan just outside Mt. Pleasant. He lived at Clare. Mt. Pleasant is the location of Central Michigan

University, and he has had some affiliation with their School of Social Work.

"He's also a gentleman farmer. He has property just outside of Clare, Michigan, about 250 acres and he has a business that is called Jerry Schmiedicke and Daughters. He had a son who died shortly after birth, named Joseph, after me. That was tough on Pam, his wife, but they eventually overcame that and had two other children, Elizabeth and Jessica. Jessica, as a matter of fact just completed her master's degree in regional planning here at the University of Wisconsin, Madison. So we've kept in touch very closely. On Jerry's little farm, he started out raising cattle for Swift and Company, until they closed in Chicago. Then he decided that his forty acres of maple trees should produce maple syrup. He's an entrepreneur. He went to Canada and studied what they do up there and came back with three or four of these large boiler units, distillers for his business, and that has been very lucrative to him.

"But what he has found most interesting was working with Mennonite farmers. They, of course, have their own general farming, but they raise, in that area of Michigan, Percherons, the huge draft horses. So, wouldn't you know it, Jerry is a Percheron farmer. He uses the big draft horses to do most of his work, and he works with the Mennonites. He helps them in the sense that they don't drive, so he helps families get to hospitals or care like that. And, they work with him in a lot of the work that is done in the fields with the maple syrup business. When he started that affiliation about twenty years ago we used to visit him at his farm up there during the summer, and the kids were absolutely fascinated with that. But it gave us another opportunity also to look at another religious organization and family oriented organization and to see the way in which the Mennonites lived and maintained their social labyrinth. I think that's been a growth experience for me and for my children. Those are good influences.

"Tom was the next sibling in birth order. Tom, too, came to the seminary. Tom lasted three years and decided it was not for him. Tom was very independent. At any rate, Tom was a very independent individual. He stayed in high school at Catholic Central and then went into working with my father and grandfather for awhile. Eventually he too felt that teaching was a road for him to explore as a career, so he finished his undergraduate work at Aquinas College, another contact with the Dominicans. I used to go out and visit him out there at Aquinas.

"At the time he was there a cousin of mine, Joyce Jacobs, who entered the Grand Rapids Dominicans. Joyce's mother was my mother's sister. Tom would often see Joyce on the campus because she was at the mother house which was just a half mile down the road from Aquinas. He would invite me out with him occasionally to just socialize with Joyce and that's when I got more involved in the Aquinas experience. That was reinforced later on. Today Tom is an evangelical, a teacher and a great gardener.

I'm talking about all these siblings and the ways in which they built a kind of relationship to the Dominican experience. I think that kind of set the stage for when I went to Catholic University. One of the places that became very attractive, particularly because of a couple of my instructors at Catholic University, was the Dominican House of Studies right across the street. I lived at Theological College at 401 N. Michigan Ave and the next northeastern large building was the Dominican House of Studies. We would often go over there for seminar meetings with some of our instructors from the School of Philosophy at Catholic University. So, it was comfortable to go there and be able to talk about Aquinas College in Grand Rapids and my cousin who was in the Grand Rapids Dominicans at the time.

"After Tom is Mary. Mary is my oldest sister, the oldest girl in the family, and she is an interesting individual. You know, there are a lot of different personalities in my family. Mary was never interested in school, never. She was interested more in her social life, and she was not real interested in any of the studies she had or anything like that. As a matter of fact, one day I was home for a vacation, and she came home and she said, 'Joe, what's a copilot?' (pronounce this like cop a lot) And I said, 'a copilot?' 'Yes, it's in one of the stories I have to read at school and I don't know what a copilot is.' And I said, 'Well, why don't you get the dictionary out?' 'Don't you know what a copilot is?' And I said, 'No, how do you spell it?' 'C-o-p-i-l-o-t.' 'Mary, that's a co-pilot.' 'What?' 'It's a copilot.' 'No, it's a co-pilot.' 'No it's a copilot.' 'Get the dictionary!' So we finally settled that issue, and we found out that a copilot is really one of those pilots that helps the pilot. This is Mary.

"Mary did not go on to college, was not interested in it and after high school went into the banking business in Grand Rapids as a teller. Maybe she was following the influence of her Uncle Robert, my dad's younger brother, who was an accountant and who has published accounting textbooks. Robert at that time was just coming out of the military and he went to work for the RC Allen Company which was a major international accountant machine business, and he helped Mary first get a position in one of the banks in town. He then interested her in at least taking some courses at Davenport Institute, which was something similar to what here in Madison is Madison Area Technical College. Bob eventually became president of Davenport and Davenport eventually became a system of colleges similar to MATC through southern Michigan and northern Indiana. At any rate, Mary was never academically inclined but was most interested in applying all of her gifts. She was natively intelligent and very much, I would say, a butterfly on a lot of things. But she was always a great spirit in the family and still is. She still lives in Grand Rapids and quit working at about the age of 45 or so because she and her husband have done very well.

"Linda was, as I was growing up, probably the last of the siblings that I knew really well. Linda went all the way through high school, did not go to college, but went to the radiology training program at St. Mary's Hospita,l and was thrilled that she was going through a program at the same institution where her mother had received her RN. At the time, because of family and church connections, she knew virtually everybody at the hospital. And she has continued to this day as an employee of St. Mary's Hospital and works in the radiology department. She started out in X-Rays and now is in CT scan and things like that. I was talking to her not too long ago and she said, 'You know one of the most difficult things I had to do was Dad's radiology treatments and his CT scan when they discovered a lymphoma that had probably been growing for ten years they guessed.' And unfortunately she was the radiologist for his radiation therapy. I say unfortunately, because he died of the treatment and not of the disease. It was one of those situations where the treatment perforated his stomach and he got an infection and died rather rapidly.

"I would call her the consoler in the family. She's been great at that. She keeps in touch with me because she wants to know about my situation with Parkinson's. It's good to keep in touch over that with her because I think she's still exploring, in dad's case, if she could have done anything differently. But, I think we reassured her on that and after all, my parents lived well into their 80's, so they had a full life. Her husband, Roger, died at the age of 38 of uncontrolled melanoma. He had, they think, picked it up when he was in the Navy and when they lived in a kind of rotating military situation. She accompanied him to Great Lakes for a couple of years and then went back to St. Mary's. We had spent a lot of time together when he died, so I talked to her about problems and issues that she was having adjusting to it. But I think again she, her children and family were heavily influenced by the church in Grand Rapids and by her family ties.

6

MY SIBLINGS: THE YOUNGER SIX SUE ANN, BILL, AND DONNA, RITA, PAUL AND RUTH

Quinque, sex, septem, octo, novem, decem
Five, six, seven, eight, nine, ten

"After that I get into the next child and the next girl is Sue Ann. Sue Ann is the one child that is outside the family circle at the present time. That is due, we think, to a major injury that she received as a result of the business that she and her husband were in raising Arabian horses. Unfortunately one day she fell off the horse and was trampled. And she suffered a severe head injury at that time. For whatever reason, at that point, she became alienated from the family. Bill was the next sibling, and Bill had good relationships with Sue, and he's tried to talk to her and it just…whatever…we don't know what's happened, but something has happened and she's the one who has alienated herself from the family. It's a task that we continue to work on and probably will for all the rest of our lives.

"What's a little bit difficult about that is that in her earlier life before the accident, we had some very, very wonderful times together. My children knew her very well when they were young. Lisa, my third child, was absolutely overcome by all of these horses. She just loved the horses. And my daughter Mary, about maybe three or four years ago, found some old film that we had, old super eight film, and unbeknown to us she took all these little ribbons of film and had them put into a video that she gave to all of us last year. Lisa said, 'Oh, why can't we get Sue back?' Some of the clips show Lisa on the horses riding and at that time she's about six or seven years old. You know, families have a lot of different experiences and probably one of the most challenging ones that we face is Sue's alienation from the family.

"Bill's the talker in the family. Bill is also a graduate of Aquinas College. He went on to the University of Michigan for his master's degree. For a while he taught mathematics at West Catholic Central. The city had grown and so had the Catholic community; so that Catholic Central established another school on the west side of Grand Rapids, and he taught at West Catholic for a number of years. And then he became very interested in working for not-for-profit organizations and fund raisers. For twenty-five years he worked in Monaghan and Associates and eventually bought the business and is presently CEO. Over the course of twenty-five years he has raised 715 million dollars for not-for-profit organizations, schools, hospitals. He's done a lot of work in the Grand Rapids area and is very well known particularly for the Van Andel family, the family that owns the Amway products. He's been very successful; he's done a lot of work with Steel Case in Grand Rapids which is one of the big office furniture producers. He also, amazingly enough, without any influence from me, did the fundraising for the Salvation Army in Madison, Wisconsin, when the Salvation Army was going to take over the buildings that American Family was freeing up after building their new campus out east of Madison.

"He came to town one day and he says, 'You know…we got to go out to eat. Where's the best steak place for a great steak?' I said, 'Well there's a little place over here on University Avenue.' We went over to University Avenue, to Smokeys, and we were having dinner and two or three people came in and they said, 'Well, Hi, Bill, how are you doing?' And Bill says, 'Now this is my brother, Joe.' And Dave Hanson said, 'Yah, I know him.' Small world! It was interesting, but Bill has been very successful and has done a lot of work in Wisconsin as well as Michigan. He's done a lot in the Fox River Valley for fundraising, most recently for the University of Wisconsin at Green Bay for their performing arts facility. Bill, as I say, is the talker of the family. He's very outgoing, very socially adept, and I keep saying, Bill, if you can't make peace with Sue, nobody can, and he's just not been able to do that.

"When my parents died they left their home and two houses near them that they owned to the family, and the family decided that Bill would take over the management of the homes. It was Bill that found a box in the basement of the house that had the woodworking industry's records in it and we were going through it not too long ago. Jerry, our brother, works with him from time to time on some things around the house.

"Donna would be after Bill in the family. Donna, now Donna Stelzer, is a business woman, the executive vice president of mortgaging in Iowa for Wells Fargo. She came to Edgewood for one year and had an unfortunate experience. It was one of the unfortunate experiences of the family, but the interesting thing I think about this is that the family came around pretty well, you know, and helped her and it's been a source of, I believe, support and really probably one of the best expressions that one can have of values, family values, religious values, influence of the church and so on. She got a lot of help from the priests and sisters of St. James in Grand Rapids at the time and her mother being a nurse helped her through a lot of it as well. Donna is the divorced mother of two children.

"Rita is next in the family. Rita is the Mary, but not quite as ebullient. Rita was not interested in school and could not have been, I think, under any circumstances, motivated to further academic work beyond high school. But, sufficiently intelligent again enough that she ,too, with the help of her uncle Robert, went into the banking business in Grand Rapids and has been in the banking business for now almost 30 years. She lives in the home where I grew up for the first five years of my life, the home that was owned by my grandfather and grandmother.

"The house itself is kind of interesting because it was a one story house when my grandfather first moved into it with his mother, Rosa, and his wife Margaret. As the family grew, Grandpa decided that they did not want to move out of the neighborhood. They had been with the church for so long, and it was close by, only two blocks down the road. And, besides, our three ethnic…I mean, that's not the words he used…but our three grocery stores were within walking distance. And, I think Rita appreciates that. The grocery stores are all gone, but the church is still there and the affiliation with the church and the school is still there and she and her children have gone there and she likes the home. My grandfather said, 'You know, we're going to stay here.' So he lifted the house up. He raised the roof, built another floor underneath it and that's the house that I knew. I knew the house once it had been raised and reinforced. The house was also constructed in such a way that the basement was really a workshop for him.

"The basement now is really a family room, probably more than that, but when I was growing up it was the site of all of the 'restricted work days because of weather place.' And my grandfather would plan that. The saws, for instance, all had to be sharpened but you couldn't take time to do the sharpening of the saws on a sunny day because that's the day that you're going to be up on roof putting on shingles or whatever. So the basement was the workshop for all that sort of thing and I spent a lot of time down there watching him with his file and some pincher that he had that would offset the teeth of the saw. They would do all of their own saw sharpening and everything like that. That's where they sharpened all the chisels for the woodworking. That was a manual operation back then. It was absolutely fascinating and I can still see him sitting there in his little chair with his vice that held the saw, and he would be going back and forth with his file and then his pinching tool.

And, I've told Rita, 'You know how the spirit of all that's going on down there yet, and I don't care if you sit down there and watch television, but Grandpa is down there sharpening his saw.' And she said, 'You know, there are times when I wonder…what was going on in this house back 50-60 years ago?' So Rita lives there. She is now a Schmiedicke who has become Short. She's Rita Short, and the mother of two children. Her husband works in the metal stamping business in Grand Rapids, and they've had a nice life together.

"Paul is the youngest boy and the second to the last of the siblings. Paul was kind of a free spirit, too, and was not academically inclined. Paul did go to the seminary for one year. But he became eventually interested in what his father and grandfather had done, at least one part of it, and that was the lumber business. Eventually he worked his way up from a stock boy in one of the lumber companies in Grand Rapids to the purchaser for them in all the Canadian connections for lumber. He knows trees and lumber quality and is just amazing, in the most thorough way I've ever seen anybody. All of his background in that is experiential with some training in special programs that were held by the lumber companies for their employees. He's never had a formal education beyond high school. He travels to Canada. He does all of the selection of the hardwoods for the furniture industry that is still partly left in Grand Rapids. Baker, for instance, is one of them. You'll notice the name, Monsignor Baker and Baker Furniture. Monsignor Baker, the pastor of our parish, St. James, was out of the Baker Furniture family. Paul has worked now for almost 20 years in that business, very successful. We often hold our reunions either at Paul's place or at Jerry's farm. Paul has a huge home on a lake in western Michigan between Grand Rapids and Muskegan. The interior of the home is, from my point of view, a showcase of virtually every piece of lumber, I think, samples of lumber that Canada produces. He's still working on the house. Last year he was working on changing the flooring in one of the rooms to a new redwood, not the redwood of California. It's a red wood, and it's kind of in the oak family, and this is his dining room. He does all the work himself. He's redoing the floors in that wood. But, every room in the house is, in some way or another, a study of different types of wood that he carefully chooses. He selects the wood both for the grain and the color, and it's really kind of a living display of all the wood products of Canada that you see there. So I think maybe the construction industry has had an influence on him.

"Ruth is the youngest. Ruth is a Bill…she's a talker. She's very outgoing, not academically inclined like Bill is. However when she finished high school, she went into the restaurant business, and she's been very successful at that. You may have heard of Zondervan's. Zondervan's is the Christian publisher in Grand Rapids. She does most of the food service for them and several of their stores. They're kind of like a Border's, you know, and they have food service within the bookstores. And in Grand Rapids, Michigan, she is the manager of their entire food service system. She has had the roughest physical limitations of anyone in the family with many, many allergies and one of them that she suffered through for a long time as a child is a fish allergy. Fortunately, medical practice has moved ahead, and that's been somewhat alleviated for her. All she had to do was smell fish being cooked, and she would just turn red as a beet with all kinds of little red rashes all over her body when she was a child. But she's lived through all of that and is doing very well. She has two of her own children. She lived within three to four blocks of my parent's home and from time to time, I'd help my dad. We'd go over to visit her in Grand Rapids and he'd say, 'You know, Ruth needs a little bit of help with the fence around her house so if you don't mind, join me, we'll go over and we'll rebuild the fence.' So we rebuilt the fence and then we rebuilt the kitchen and then we rebuilt the…but we had fun helping Ruth upgrade her house over the years.

"As I've talked about my family life and my siblings, I've given them titles, or described what I think are their outstanding characteristics. So, in fairness, I should probably do the same for myself. I think I can characterize myself as the literary person in the family. I'll share a bit of a story behind that. When I was in the 7th grade at St. James School in Grand Rapids, one of the

Sisters had a club, the St. James Literary Club. One day I was called into the Principal's Office. I was a bit fearful, thinking I had done something wrong. As it turned out, I was being called in to be asked if I would be the president of the Literary Club. And I asked for time to think about that. They gave me two days.

"I went home asked my mother what it would mean to be president of the Literary Club. 'Well, that would be wonderful. You'd get involved in a lot of reading, I'm sure. And probably some writing. You do that pretty well. I have a friend that's in the Westside literary club. I'll have you talk with her.' I did, and it jived pretty well with my interests. I liked to read stories, and poetry. I took that, and for two years I was president of the St. James Literary Club. So I think that set me on a track that not only differentiated me from my siblings. But it also set me on a direction that steered me away from my father's and grandfather's desire that I enter the construction business, as well as my other grandfather's desire that I enter the pharmacy business. Neither of those career choices melded very well with my literary interests.

"But, back to the family; our communications, I think, are just fascinating and the opportunity to see that happening within the family is great. We have regular reunions to gather us all together. It was at one of those reunions by the way, you know it's fascinating to look at what happens to families, the year when I was diagnosed with Parkinson's in '04, and in the summer of '05 we had a reunion at my brother's home at the lake. And that was Paul's house. We were just talking and Jerry had been asking me what was happening with my Parkinson's and what I was doing with it. I told him I was going to be going on an experimental drug here in Wisconsin, and it was coming up for approval, but hadn't quite been approved. He was just asking me what some of the risks were. And I got talking about how it limits some of the things you can eat because rasaduline interacts with tyramines and the tyramines are very prominent in anything that's aged, so like aged cheese, parmesan cheese, pepperoni. After our conversation was over Jerry started talking with, at that time, the four year-old, Andrew, my grandson from Pennsylvania. Jerry said, 'I hear you're going up to visit Grandpa.' 'Yes, I am.' 'Are you going to have fun over there?' 'I don't know, Grandpa can't eat any of the good stuff.' He had been listening to the conversation. But I thought, here he is talking about good stuff and I suspect this is the influence of the Pizza Hut ads that he sees on TV because I'm talking about all the things that go on a good pizza. 'Oh, Grandpa can't eat any of the good stuff.' So he wasn't sure he was going to have any fun. Maybe Grandpa wouldn't let him have pizza…that was one of his favorite foods, by the way. We'd say to Andrew, 'Andrew, what would you like for lunch?' 'Pizza!'

7

INFLUENCE OF CHURCH

Te Deum Laudamus. **We praise you, God.**

"The opportunities that I think family and church offered were really the framing scaffold of my early life. In the center of our lives were family and church, and we were two blocks from St. James Church, which was our parish. It was the site of a long time relationship between my grandfather and the church as well. He had lived in the neighborhood there since he was born in 1885. The church offered many opportunities for growth and development I think that were reinforced by the family, and the values of both were shared. My father and my grandfather were both significant members of the church there. They came from a construction background, and in addition to their own businesses, they managed to spend some time in all the little projects at the church as well. I learned the business very early but also left the business for some reasons I'll talk about later on. The sisters who staffed St. James School, the parochial school at St. James Church, were School Sisters of Notre Dame, and I attended St. James School. My affiliation with the Dominicans, who were present in Grand Rapids at Aquinas College, and later at Edgewood College, comes a little later.

"My decision to go to the seminary--that's one of those things that was partially conscious and partially unconscious. But we had such a connection with the church as a kind of central social activity for the family that there was a lot of influence from both the sisters in the school and the priests in the parish to eventually go into the seminary. And there were a couple other things, I believe, that carried influence not consciously on my part but on my parents' part. A decision had to be made at the end of grade school as to whether or not you would go into Catholic Central High School or whether you'd go into Union High School which was our area public high school. And my parents were thinking I might go to Union High School. We went to a meeting with the counselors at Union High School who told my mother that her son should really be going into the vocational track because he comes from a construction family, and he really probably would not do very well in the college prep program. Well my parents thought otherwise, and their wisdom prevailed.

"I want to talk a little bit about my parents' wisdom and insights. By the time I was in 8th grade there were several younger children at home. My father's education was through high school, with additional training in architectural drawing, draftsmanship and what today I think we'd call operations management, how to run a business, how to manage planning and scheduling for construction…things like that. My mother's was a two-year RN program at St. Mary's Hospital in Grand Rapids, Michigan. As a result, both of my parents knew the value of good education and how to direct their children.

"Mother thought that it might be better that maybe we go and talk with the Fathers and with the Sisters and see whether or not the seminary is something that would be good for you because you would get an excellent education. And so we did that and the pastor of our parish, St. James in Grand Rapids, was Monsignor Baker, Raymond E. Baker, and he had been there as long as I knew at that time. He was a wonderful old man and he would, on occasion when the priest's house was vacant because they were going to meetings or whatever, call on me to come and sit and answer the phone. So I became very involved with the priest there. The Sisters started me on the altar boy/acolyte track in the first grade, and I was deeply involved in all that. As a matter of fact one of the things I remember very well from those days was when I was a little bit older in the 6th, 7th, and 8th grades, I was to be the special altar boy for the Mass that was held for the Sisters in the chapel in their own convent. And I would go into the convent early in the morning, one day a week, about 5 o'clock in the morning. And as I'd go in the front door I could smell the toast and the coffee and the oatmeal being prepared for breakfast after the Mass. It was always a very positive experience. Out of those influences, at any rate, came an eventual decision to enter

St. Joseph's Seminary in Grand Rapids, Michigan, which was the diocesan seminary.

"I think that's one of the important things about a school, a Catholic School or a public school, that's a neighborhood school, where the families are known over periods of time, and the students are known over periods of time, and there's a context in which they are understood by the teachers and administrators. I think of that from time to time, and situations today, where kids are bussed for a long period of time, out of their neighborhood, and not known. So that was very important for me, and the teachers reinforced my gifts. That was significant in setting a course for me in finding my own strengths. I think it's helped to nurture my personal strength and determination, to set deep roots, moving my family and me into a choice of high school, and ultimately, life choices.

"My model for strength began with my father, and the way they treated tuberculosis in those days, and my mother's support for him. His lungs had been collapsed in half, so he was living with that as a permanent condition. He had been told he probably wouldn't live past 30. He was always susceptible to pneumonia, the flu, that was a constant struggle. My parents put a great deal of faith in their prayer life, in their church life, in their commitment to each other. That was a very strong influence on some determinative issues in me. It allowed me to see the possibilities. At the time, not consciously for me, but as I look back on it, I can see the influence.

"My father had a great devotion to Our Lady of Perpetual Help, and attended the weekly devotions at our church. I think that was a sign that it was necessary to look for help in difficulty. That faith of his became a milestone for me, a great consolation, a great reassurance. I don't think I thought deeply about it then, but looking back, it was a constant in my life.

"Another fact about my father was that he was strongly committed to what we would call today service or community-based learning. Back then we called it the spiritual and corporal works of mercy. He was very committed to helping those who had less than we did. And he did that through the St. Vincent De Paul Society. And part of our day on Saturdays when I was working for him, was going to the local SVDP Society. In Grand Rapids, it was a kind of mini Los Angeles, with lots of burning of buildings, where the needy lived. We would do a lot of things. Sometimes they needed things repaired. We would do that, and donate all the supplies. His sons who worked with him donated their time, sometimes reluctantly, because they wanted to be at a football game. There was a significance that didn't engage us until later in life, but we recognized there a very strong orientation to service, the corporal works of mercy. Sometimes we were called to sort clothes, set out new deliveries, help out the store manager.

"We spent a lot of time when the church needed something. I recall spending two Saturdays putting the racks that would hold the hymnals into the pews. We had built the racks, and my brother and I installed them. It was an example of the close tie between the church and the family. I'm very grateful for that today. It was a challenge then.

8

SEMINARY LIFE AT ST. JOSEPH'S HIGH SCHOOL AND JUNIOR COLLEGE

Consensu Omnium **By the agreement of everyone**

"It would be high school and two years of junior college. I didn't know until late in my adult life that the rector of the seminary, Monsignor Belicki, was a student at the Catholic University in Washington D.C. It was really his influence, I understand now, and his relationship with the Bishop of Grand Rapids, Bishop Haas, who started the School of Social Work at Catholic University, that there came a recommendation to send me as a representative of the diocese of Grand Rapids to Catholic University for my bachelor's degree and master's degree in a program that's known as the Basselin Scholars Program. A special scholarship had been established by a lumber magnate from northern New York who was upset with the way that preaching was occurring in churches. He felt that the Catholic University, as the Pontifical University of the United States, should provide some leadership in a program that trained future priests in preaching and in careful preparation of their sermons, writing and so on. So I became nominated for and eventually was sent to Catholic University for bachelors and masters study, as part of that program.

"I attended the seminary for six years in Grand Rapids, completing high school and junior college. During the final two years there, I now realize that the administration of the school was arranging for me to attend Catholic University.

"I want to summarize maybe some of the lessons, some beliefs and values that are strong and influential in my life, some particular life lessons that have given me that foundation. It's the influence of family, yes, but it's also the tie of the family to a larger community. And those things are all important, and I think at the bottom of it, what it does, is it builds an understanding of respect. It builds an understanding of the limits both of one individual and one family. I think it builds a respect of the spirit of a larger community influence whether it's a church, for us it was definitely the church, the influence there was very strong. And I think that one of the people that really started that, now that I look back, because I did not know her that well, is Rosa.

"Rosa, my great grandmother, must have been a very strong individual…that's all I can say. She met my great grandfather

Schmiedicke in Manitowoc, Wisconsin, when he was there for some work. He was a saddler at that time before he went to Michigan to build. They were what, in the old Church, we would call a mixed marriage. She was a very strong Catholic. He was a very strong German Lutheran. They had to leave Wisconsin. That's the way it was in those days.

"I didn't know any of this until much later in life. As a matter of fact, I didn't learn the details until after my parents had died, so I can't follow up on some of these things. I had started my genealogy research, and I told my dad I was doing it. And he said, 'Well you know, that's great, but you may find out some things you don't want to know.' And I said, 'Well, have you got any ideas about what those might be?' 'No, but' he says 'I'm just telling you, that if you get into this you may be surprised.' In some respects I'm surprised, because when I was growing up, there was no other history of the family but a Catholic history. I mean, it was not spoken or acknowledged in any way.

"But as I look into it further and further, I realize, from my perspective, how important the German Lutheran experience was to that piece of the Schmiedicke family, and how much similarity there was in the reinforcement of the German Lutheran experience to the family as there was of the Catholic experience. It also reinforces the idea of the linkages between a family and a church because a couple of the Schmiedickes in Manitowoc were part of the First German Lutheran Church of Manitowoc, were elders on the board. And they supported a lot of what I think today we would call social support network, safety nets. My father did the same in his work with the Catholic Church in Michigan. All of those values come out, and they become influential in family circumstances.

"We were driving through Manitowoc one time in the early '60s from Madison to the boat as we called it, the ferry that went across from Manitowoc to Muskegon at that time, and then Ludington. And we were driving down one of the streets on the way to the boat, and we passed a business, and the name of the business was Schmiedicke Battery Company. And I was absolutely fascinated with that because the name was spelled exactly the same way as we spell it. So when we came back I stopped and went into the business and said, 'Is there a Schmiedicke around here?' 'Well, no, you know they're not really tied up with the business anymore, they've kind of retired, and one of them has moved to North Dakota, and one of them is down in Florida. There's really no Schmiedickes left in town. We bought the business and the name.' I didn't get very far with that, and I didn't do much on genealogy at that time. That always stuck in my head, and it prompted me eventually to look further and see what the relation was because there was a story within the family that my great grandfather and his wife, Rose, walked across Lake Michigan on the frozen ice one winter. I don't know if that's true or not, but that was a story that was told…that's how they came to Michigan.

"I graduated from St. James Grade School, and then I went on to St. Joseph Seminary, in Grand Rapids. This would be a challenge because it was the first time I was away from home for any extended period. We're talking not more than six miles from home. I was wondering what would happen. I'd be gone for six months. In those days, the seminary was a relatively closed environment. The only contact those of us who lived in town could have was through our laundry, which our family could pick up on Saturday, and deliver back two weeks later. And what was very exciting was you could get a note from your family in your laundry, and you might also get a little bag of cookies, although you weren't supposed to. So you could look forward to those. It was a whole different world, it was an eye opener for me, I encountered a lot of different kinds of people. Since they were all Catholic, you would assume they would have similar values, but they didn't.

"Part of it was social class, ethnic in the European tradition; there were no blacks or Hispanics, all European, but great differentiation, Italian, German, Irish. The other thing that I think was very different for me was that it was a very strong patriarchal experience, all men. We had worked for my father, and there was a dimension of that at home, but there was a lot of influence from my mother at home, in my life at least. That existed at the seminary only in the sense that the Sisters maintained the kitchen. They did all the cooking, baking, but they were relatively isolated from our experience, unless we were in the dishroom. I worked in the dishroom quite a bit, so the environment on a day-to-day basis was mostly men. So that was different from what I was used to at home.

"What I think about were relationships on the social level. There were a lot of good things in the seminary, it was fairly well structured, it was good for me to have a time to study, to pray, to go to class, to go to bed. I compare this experience with that of my siblings. In the seminary, everybody attended all the liturgies, in the old tradition. At the same time, there was a lot of excitement in the liturgical practices. I became involved in the choir. I didn't realize that I had a singing voice. I should have expected it, with my mother playing the organ. My grandfather Ernie performed in skits and musicals at St. James as well. I got involved in choir and performed in musicals, like the Mikado. Those were great opportunities.

"I was terribly honored to be asked in my high school senior year to be the editor of the school newspaper. There was a young man in his last year at the seminary who took me aside for about a week, while everyone else went out to play football. He would ask me to write an article prior to our meeting. He'd go through it word by word, who, what, when, where, can you say it differently? Basically, he trained me in journalism, without a course, a great learning experience, because I began to learn how to tell a story, how to use a picture to tell a story.

"A few things happened at the seminary, although it probably was not so exciting to the world at large: we got a television, so we could watch Bishop Fulton J. Sheen. I was absolutely mystified by his oratorical skills, and challenged myself to be like him. I don't know if I ever was. Mike Lyberger, an Edgewood colleague, once said of me, 'He's the only one on the faculty who writes and speaks like Cicero.' I never heard Cicero.

"The seminary experience always ended in June, and there was a relief that one was going home and reentering family life. That got more and more difficult, largely because the expectation was that I would work during the summer in the family construction business, and I had some interest in doing some other things. But, I got through it. My summers were spent in construction work, and helping in the family business, offering quite a change from seminary life during the year.

"We had a very large study hall, about 160 students, all in one room, studying in silence. If one had to go to the men's room, it was a quiet walk to the proctor who sat in the corner, surveying it all. One would be grilled on whether such a trip was absolutely necessary. Study hall also offered the availability of the priests on the seminary staff to talk about various dispositions of being a priest. One of them went something like this: 'There is no royal road to knowledge. All alike must travel the same rocky road.' I think about that from time to time, because it was a rocky road. There were some kids who were having an easier time than I was, but I think there was an attempt to build a common understanding of the life of study and preparation for priesthood.

"The other common experience that had an impression on me was that we had the readings during meals, an old monastic tradition. That opened a whole new book in my life, because there were things read to us that I wouldn't have encountered otherwise. I mentioned that Bishop Haas was the bishop of Grand Rapids, at the time I was growing up. He had a very strong social community orientation, particularly to justice and equality. As a result, there were frequent readings from his published materials. I am fascinated, thinking back, about how much influence he placed on the individual's experience in a religious context, in contrast to the growing interest on corporate culture. There was one reading about white bread. He thought that this was an experience that wouldn't be good for us. He said, 'They process everything out of the basic grain, and they try to put it back in it, and there is something lost in the natural cycle.' This was in the 1950's. There were also excerpts in his writings about labor unions. He also had a reputation as an outstanding labor negotiator. And he was recognized by the federal government for that. So the mealtime readings in the cafeteria opened up another whole book or author that had a strong influence on me.

"My father had come home one day complaining about a family that had been close friends with my grandfather, and our family construction company had just finished doing some work for them. They would not pay their bills. And he thought it was a violation of their friends, of their commonly shared religious beliefs, and democratic principles. He said, 'Joe, would you help me write a letter to Johnny Guest?' I helped him write the letter, and it was relatively easy because I had heard all those writings of Bishop Haas. In fact I turned to his book to help me write the letter. He had a written a book on principles of sociology when he was working at the Catholic University. It was those experiences that began to shape my life, working at St. Vincent de Paul, being named president of the Literary Club at St. James, certainly a widening experience in my life, and a shaping, a formation was taking place at the same time.

"The seminary was run by the Diocese of Grand Rapids. I was there for six years, four years of high school and two years of junior college. By the time I went to college, they had constructed a separate building, and that building became the focal point for both the residential and academic experience. We still participated in the liturgical experience at the general chapel. And we still occasionally had class in the old building. There began to be a differentiation for the college experience from the high school experience. With that, the seminary used the college students as mentors, today we'd call them peer advisors, to run groups with the high school seminarians.

"And, college students ran work teams. I headed up a work team, and we had a section of the campus to shovel snow. There were no snow plows. We would go out at 6:30 am, and shovel the semi-circular drive, the north portion, from the door down to Burton St., and clean that up. At times we would line up, 13 wide, and push the snow. Light fluffy snow would work that way. That experience began to give us the role of older students vs. younger students, good leadership experiences as well.

"The curriculum of the seminary was heavily literary, though we had science. Mr. Filardo stands out as one of those wonderful teachers who came in to teach science, since there were no qualified priests. We should have had Fr. Samuel Mazzuchelli (founder of the Sinsinawa Dominicans, and esteemed scientist.) His classroom was organized with cigar boxes. "Mr. Schmiedicke, you know that the bunson burners are in box marked Bunson Burners.'

"The other classes were heavily reading and writing oriented. Occasionally there were those like Father Bill who would give us topics like 'There are turkeys, and there are turkeys. I'd like 250 words on that.' I thought, there must be many types of turkeys, white turkeys, wild turkeys. I went to the encyclopedia. This primed the creative pump. The material was different.

"The curriculum was fairly standardized across most seminaries at the time; we had Greek, Latin, and English, composition, rhetoric, prose, poetry, Joyce Kilmer. And the material of the courses offered the opportunity for substantially new experiences. We had to memorize Greek: *'Andramoi ennepe.'* Greek started in high school. At St. Joseph's, I had six years of Latin and four years of Greek. By the time most of us left St. Joseph's Seminary, we were pretty well versed in Greek and Latin, to the extent that when I attended Catholic University, I took but one additional course in Latin. When I reached the University of Wisconsin for my PhD, 15 years after attending Catholic University, 20 years after St. Joseph's Seminary, it was no challenge to present Classical Languages in addition to French. By the time I left St. Joseph's Seminary, I had studied three languages.

9

THEOLOGICAL COLLEGE AT CATHOLIC UNIVERSITY OF AMERICA

Credo ut intelligam **I believe that I may understand**

St. Augustine

"The next expectation in my educational path was to move on to the major seminary in Detroit. In my case I didn't realize until June of my graduation year, that I was being considered for a scholarship to Catholic University, and didn't find out about it until it was announced at the graduation ceremony; so I didn't know I was going and didn't fully understand what that was all about. I wondered what it would be like? I hadn't left Grand

Rapids much, and here I was going to Washington, D.C., the national capital. Is this something that fits into my qualifications? It was a very exciting moment, and I didn't realize the significance of it.

"It was also a challenge to my family because they knew what it would mean. I think it was probably one of the prayerful moments for my mother and father because I had helped out a lot in the business; I was probably what would today be called the Operations Manager, and did a lot of scheduling of the work and carrying out of tasks. That was all going to be challenged by this scholarship, clearly an honor and clearly a challenge.

"There have been two basilicas in my life. The first was St. Adalberts in Grand Rapids, the Polish National Church. We used to go because it was the only church in town with Mass at about 4:30 am, and my mom would begin her work as a nurse at 7:00 am so she would go, and occasionally I would accompany her.

"When I arrived in Washington D.C., the second basilica appeared, and that was the National Shrine of the Immaculate Conception. Oddly enough it wasn't as inspiring as many of the great cathedrals of Europe, but it *was* the National Shrine. It was located on the campus of Catholic University, and across the street from my home away from home, the Theological College at 401 North Michigan Avenue. The Shrine at that time had not been finished. The lower level had been open since the 1940's for Mass, and looked, I thought, the way catacombs would look. The heavy stonework that marked the walls of the basement church was rather awe inspiring. I don't believe I had ever attended church in anything like that. The church itself was under construction while I was there. In 1958, it was sufficiently completed that it was going to be consecrated. About 50 students from the Theological College were going to be involved in the service. Fr. Walter Schmitz, who taught liturgical courses at the Theological College, and ultimately had a chair in Religious Studies and Theology named for him at Catholic University, was an outstanding liturgist. He served as Master of Ceremonies for the Archbishop and for various dignitaries that would come to DC for various services.

"One of the roles I played for the Consecration Ceremony was 'seating the Kennedys,' Robert and his wife, Ted and his wife. I don't think I understood the full implication of this event, making connections with them. The Church was full at that ceremony, and one of the most impressive liturgical experiences I've ever had. Nothing every duplicated it. It was an absolutely beautiful day, unusual for DC. Usually DC has a lot of humidity, but it was not humid at all that day.

"The scholarship I received was from Catholic University, the Basselin Scholars Program. Mr. Basselin was a lumber magnate in upper New York State in the 19th Century, and set a scholarship in place at Catholic University, to prepare priests to give good sermons. It was a heavily literary program. There was an individual in place to give guidance from the speech side, Fr. Madden. He was a member of the American Shakespeare Society and held a class in the basement of the theater at Catholic University. In the first class there were 12 of us, meeting in a basement, with windows at ground level, across a grassy knoll from Maryknoll. This little man, bald as a billiard ball, in his black suit didn't say a word as we came in the door. When we were seated, he rose and said: 'Gentlemen, welcome to the bowels of the earth. We have one naked light bulb, so read carefully.' That opened my eyes to what was ahead. Occasionally he would invite us to the Iron Gate Inn in DC for dinner to talk about what we had been studying. He was very immersed in his Shakespeare studies, despite the fact that there were 48 different spellings of Shakespeare's name, and whether there really was a Shakespeare. Fr. Madden provided the guidance for the Basselin students and provided the instruction for the speech side. We were enrolled as part of that scholarship in the School of Philosophy, equivalent to a major in Philosophy. We took 25-26 credits a semester.

"I came as a junior in college. They kept us busy, since seminarians have nothing else to do except to study. We did not take courses in Latin, but the courses were delivered in Latin in the School of Philosophy. For some it was a challenge. I served as what today would be called an advisor, helping people with Latin. I look back on that and see another challenge to the ideas of social class that surprised me. I also encountered wonderful people, mostly men, along with some Sisters.

"We took a course in Religious Education, and took a course in pedagogy even though it was not a formal system of preparation for a license. The residential experience was very important. I resided at the Theological College, 401 N. Michigan Avenue. The Sulpicians managed the residence. We were each assigned a Spiritual Director. I had one with one arm, who had fought in WWI, and spoke about 12 languages; he was about 85 years old when I met him. I never had an experience like that since. It was not only a Spiritual Director, but someone with general life experience, remarkably alert at 85. He died about 3 years after I left. There were remarkable people I met at Theological College, people we wouldn't have met at Catholic University. We did have delightful Pere Moan, Father Moan, a graduate of the Sorbonne, who would always talk to you in French, whether you knew French or not. I had an opportunity to practice my French with him. He was steeped in History of Philosophy and Ethics, and relating to him provided me an excellent experience outside of class to encounter strong intellectual leadership.

"The Theological College housed the Bassellin Scholars and Theology students, post masters student working on lectorates in sacred theology and doctorates. We were young guys. Catholic University offered a lot of rich experiences as a pontifical university. I got my BA there and would have gotten my MA if I had stayed there.

"There was a family event that occurred. My father got very ill in my senior year. There were a couple of other things. I had an operation on my legs my senior year. I had returned to Washington after the summer when that occurred, and I went into the hospital for two weeks. My father became very concerned, and called the seminary every day to learn my circumstances. As I think about it now, I never asked him, but he was concerned about his own health. When I returned the next fall after I received my BA I wasn't there four or five weeks, when I got a call from home that he wasn't doing well. It would be important that I come back because there was no one to run the family construction business. It was a business and a family decision for me to leave school.

"At the end of that term I struggled for a couple of months; I wasn't ready to leave Catholic University. When I came home for Christmas, I stayed and worked for probably six months to keep the business afloat. My dad recovered. I then went to teach Latin and speech at Catholic Central High School in Grand Rapids. I taught there for one semester and decided that I really liked the experience and wanted to go into school teaching.

"At Catholic University, the influence of the St. Vincent de Paul Club was deepened by 'Walks', a monthly experience when clusters of us, three or four in a group, would go out for works of mercy. We would walk for prisoners, visit jail: that experience was so powerful. That led me to a deeper understanding of legal systems in Mobile later on. Another shaping force was the governmental experience, meeting with Gerry Ford, going to his office. The other influence was the cultural experiences, since we had more opportunities to get out and see things in the community, such as the National Gallery of Art, the Medical Museum, the Smithsonian, and many others.

"While my world was greatly expanded while living in Washington, DC, there is the life question of whether priesthood was a conscious life choice. I think it was confirmed when I went to DC. It was not a conscious choice for me at the St. Joseph Seminary level. I think seminaries have improved somewhat these days. I'm not going to tell stories out of school, about the dark side, and there are some. But the seminary experience at St. Joseph Seminary was a family expectation, and I was going on to something that my mother and father felt was a better thing for me. 'The public schools are going to turn you into a vocational student, and we think you have more talent than that.' It was easy to go, because it was reinforced by the family, hard because I was leaving home for the first time. I wondered, 'What's that going to do to my relationship with my grandparents, and brothers and sisters?' It wasn't like sitting down one day and asking what am I going to do? What are the long-term implications? The movement from St. Josephs to Catholic University was a period of wondering what this would do to one's connections back home. Given that the bishop, the pastor, and my parents thought this was a good idea; maybe it is a good idea!

"I graduated from St. Joseph's Seminary Junior College in 1957, at age 20, still heavily influenced by those around me. I came home at Christmas, 1959 and stayed home. I sat down and wrote a letter to the rector of the Theological College at Catholic University, probably one of the most difficult letters I ever wrote, from the point of view of trying to get hold of whether priesthood was a conscious choice. I got a letter back from him, very positive, explaining why he thought it was a good choice. Near the end of the letter he said 'I wish I knew our seminarians better, and if I did I'd know you lived on the street called Straight. The Biblical reference to that is one that you should keep in mind.' I never thought of that in myself, being a straight thinker. I was clearly leaving one life and starting another one.

"I went on from there, and I think I made the right choice, frankly. I had a roommate from my first day that I never changed. His name was Sammy Jacobs. He was a mulatto from Louisiana, and he had a whole different experience to share. He worked very hard at his studies. He did not have the benefit I had of fine instructors. It was a rockier road for him. And Sammy is now a Bishop of the Huoma-Thibodaux Diocese of Louisiana. I went to his First Mass in Lake Charles, his home, and expressed my support. He has never written me since then. I bet if I went up to him, he would know me, and be there for me, as he had been when we were roommates. He has provided fine leadership in the Church.

10

MARQUETTE UNIVERSITY

Certe, toto, sentio nos in kansate non iam adesse

You know, Toto, I have a feeling we're not in Kansas anymore

"The transition away from home had many steps, some of them larger than others, and each step intertwined with a return home for a time. As young Joe, just a freshman in high school, I left home the first time to attend St. Joseph's High Seminary in Grand Rapids. Although the seminary was located in my home town, the rules were strict about not going home or having visitors. The exception was the student laundry box, which was sent home and returned every two weeks. Inside the laundry box, folded among the clean shirts and sox, my mother, Madeleine

Schmiedicke would tuck in a bag of homemade cookies or brownies, along with a note to her first born. I remember looking forward to these reminders of family love.

"My attendance at the seminary was balanced by summers at home, interacting with my younger siblings in the family, and working in the family business with my father and grandfather. Work in the construction business developed at least two sets of skills for me. The first was that of physical construction work, learning the building trade from the generations that preceeded me. The second skill was that of the business and accounting side of the family business. This skill was tested and exercised specifically at the time when my father was extremely ill, and I was a student at Catholic University, working on my Master's degree. I returned home for Christmas in 1959, and coming face-to-face with my father's illness and the condition of the family business, decided to stay at home and offer my assistance.

"After remaining in Grand Rapids for the completion of the academic year, I tried my hand at teaching Latin at St. Joseph's High School, my alma mater. The teaching experience, coupled with my strong and focused Catholic education thus far inspired me to undertake a career in education. Little did I imagine how extensive the impact of that decision would be on my life, and the lives of countless students! I decided that I required a Master's degree and moved to Milwaukee, Wisconsin, to attend Marquette University in 1960. This move away from Grand Rapids would be my final departure, with frequent returns to visit family; I would never live at home again.

"One of the best recommendations I could get was to Marquette. I went to Marquette University in Milwaukee in 1960, and graduated in 1962, with an M.Ed. That began the eventual relationship with education and Edgewood. I taught one year at Washington High School on the northwest side of Milwaukee. When I completed my internship with a fantastic experience there, I worked with an outstanding woman, a teacher of classics. One time we debated the relationship of the singulars and plurals in Latin and Greek and their counterparts in English. Are the agreements the same as in English? Our students thought we were nuts. We had lots of fun.

"A new chapter in my life began at Marquette University, where I enrolled in 1960, to get my teaching and administrative license. I had been teaching at a Catholic school without a license. I became rather attached to Father John Reiner, a Jesuit and professor of comparative education. He later became the President of Marquette, probably one of the most popular presidents of recent years. In February or March of 1962, after I had worked as a research assistant for two years, he called me and asked me if I was interested in some volunteer services. He asked if I was familiar with Spring Hill College in Mobile, Alabama, and I said I wasn't. The college was experiencing some trouble, had lost part of their endowment, and were looking for some people to give service in teaching, with minimal compensation: housing, food and a small stipend. He asked if I would be willing to go down in the summer of 1962 and teach. I wasn't committed to

Mary Ellen Gevelinger, O.P.

anything that summer except working with my father at home, so I responded to Father Reiner's call.

"Although I was a new graduate with a Masters of Education Degree from Marquette, there was a deeper level of real world education awaiting young me. That was a summer I'll never forget. That journey south opened up an awareness on my part of some of the issues we face in this country that I was naïve about. I left my home in Grand Rapids, Michigan, and drove to Mobile. Along the way I stopped at Jackson, Tennessee, one night and continued the two hour drive the next morning. Most of drive is through swampy, unpopulated area. As I entered one of the swampy areas, with a two lane highway and little shoulder, I came upon a group of prisoners working on reconstruction on the road. I stopped for a flagman who came up to me and asked if I had any cigarettes? 'No.' ' Got $ 5?' ' No.' 'You're going to be here a long time.' I rolled up my car window and sat for five to six minutes. Finally a car came up behind me, and both cars sat another five to six minutes. At that point another car came. Finally the flagman came up and said, 'You're very lucky.' I drove on ahead.

"The impact of that experience was transformative for Joe Schmiedicke and had a lasting effect on my future career. I thought I'd never encountered anything like that, alone on a highway, with a guard with a big shotgun. I wasn't in the North anymore; I was experiencing a cultural difference, an awareness of some of the ways that differed with black persons. I arrived in Mobile and was hosted in an apartment arranged by Springhill

College. It was one block from campus, very convenient. I was there three days and someone cut the screen out of the kitchen window in my apartment while I was teaching, and stole everything that belonged to me: my watch, books, everything. The college officials suggested I call the police. They came out and said I'd never get anything back.

"Even then, I paid attention to what was the reality of the city that hosted me that summer. A week later I read in a newspaper that the average school completion rate of the Mobile Police Department was 5th grade. They weren't very well prepared. Two weeks later I received a call. The police had a watch they thought might be mine. I was never so scared in my life as I walked into that jail with people screaming and yelling. A detective took me into a little area, and he said, 'We're trying to do something with these guys. Is this your watch?' My initials were on the back and the date of my graduation from Marquette.

"I went back to Spring Hill College and said I hoped I didn't have to do that again. The college officials had talked to Bill Sessions. He and his wife had invited me to live with them the rest of the summer, so I did, not realizing that he was connected to the Sessions family, with many political connections to the FBI, the house and senate. He was a very humble man, and appreciated his family history and the circumstances in which he lived. Later that summer just before I left Mobile, Governor George Wallace stood at the doors of the University of Alabama and said 'I will throw my body on these bayonets before I allow a black person inside these doors.' And I will never forget that."

FAMILY PHOTOS

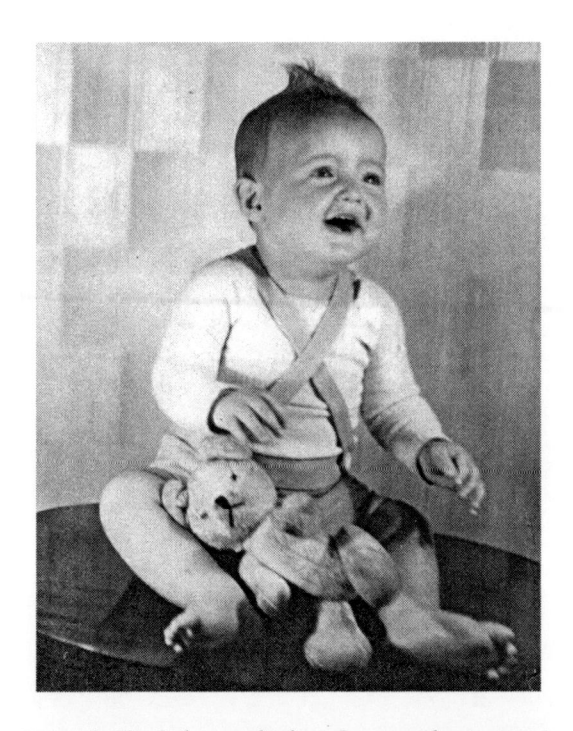

Joseph E. Schmiedicke, September, 1938

Seminarian Joseph Schmiedicke, Fall, 1958

Joseph Schmiedicke, May 1962,
graduating from Marquette University

Marian Rajani and Joseph Schmiedicke,
newly engaged, June, 1962

Wedding Day, September 1, 1962, for Joseph and Marian Rajani Schmiedicke

II

FAMILY OF CHOICE: MARRIAGE AND CHILDREN

INTRODUCTION

Stories of extended courtships and exotic proposals are the focus of many media stories. In the lore of most families, the story of meetings and courtships is usually a tale of love and determination. Sometimes those tales have the added complication of distance, financial distress, or even the demands of war. The tale of Joe and Marian, in Joe's words, came down to "brown eyes and English Class."

While attending Marquette University, Joe became friends with a beautiful young undergraduate education major, Marian Jane Rajani, from Park Ridge, Illinois. Marian was an undergrad student, and Joe was fulfilling some requirements by taking an English Class. Marian received her BS in education from Marquette University in May 1962, at the same time that Joe received his Master's degree. The two became engaged in June of 1962.

Marian was clearly smitten with this tall, handsome and charismatic young man, and decided to take action. While Joe was far away in the South during the summer of '62, Marian was feeling his absence, and decided to assert her feelings. As

Joe explains it, "she called me and said that she thought our relationship had progressed to the point where we should get married. I agreed. She also had a date in mind, September 1, 1962, just a few weeks away. I guess you'd call it a reverse proposal. Anyway, I agreed, and we were married on the date she selected, in Park Ridge, Illinois.

A first meeting in late 2008 and early 2009 with the Schmiedicke offspring was an instant view back to the visage of a young Joe and Marian. David could be mistaken for the young Joe on his graduation from Marquette, or the proud groom on his wedding day in 1962. Mary, blessed with the Schmiedicke height and facial features, has her mother's lovely olive skin. Lisa, the middle daughter, proudly wears her maternal grandmother Justina Rajani's curly hair. Megan, the youngest, strikingly resembles her mother in Joe and Marian's wedding picture. She even remarks that, as she nears the age her mother was when she died, she sees the strong resemblance.

These four adult children continue telling their family story, assisted by Cherie Schmiedicke and Marsha Callahan.

11

DAVID SCHMIEDICKE AND CHERIE SCHMIEDICKE, HIS WIFE

Dies natalis **Birthday**

David Paul was born on June 30, 1963, just days before Joe began his position at Edgewood College, in Madison, Wisconsin. He was named for his uncle Paul David, Joe's younger brother. "My mom liked that combination of names," is David's way of telling about his name. Joe recalls that Pope Paul VI was elected just a few days prior to David Paul's birth. As a way of explaining David's name, and the connection with Pope Paul VI, Cherie lovingly says of Joe, "There's a story for every occasion."

David was born in West Allis, a suburb of Milwaukee, Wisconsin. "Both parents were teaching high school, I think. Within a week of my birth we moved to Madison where my dad had a job at Edgewood College. Living in Madison- that's all I knew."

David positions himself in the Schmiedicke family history by noting that he is the oldest son, and only son in his immediate family, with three younger sisters; his dad, Joe is the oldest in his family of eleven, while Joe's dad, Edward Schmiedicke, was the oldest of his family of five siblings. David's son, Peter, is the oldest son in a family with 2 younger sisters.

Growing up around Edgewood was a part of life for the young and growing Schmiedicke family. The college is a much different place now, as the grown children reflect. David remembers seeing all the Sisters there. A fond memory is also College Christmas parties with Santa making an appearance to present gifts to the young children of newly hired lay teachers. Gradually the campus that was home to the Dominican Sisters became home to new college faculty. Michael Lybarger and Daniel Guilfoil had come to Edgewood about the same time as Joe Schmiedicke, and their families and children grew up knowing each other well.

"I went to four year old kindergarten with Sister Christina, then five year old kindergarten, and Edgewood Campus School. As the oldest in the family and only boy, I pretty much followed the rules," recalls David. Of course, the fact that all of his teachers, especially the Sisters, knew his father, was a strong deterrent to any troublesome tendencies. David remembers that about half of his teachers at the Campus School were Sisters. Thus began a tradition for the Schmiedicke children, as they all attended Edgewood preschool, kindergarten, and Campus School, just across the street from the family home on Woodrow Street in Madison.

The logical next step was attending Edgewood High School. Some Dominican Sisters were still teaching there, and the Principal was Sister Kathleen O'Connell. David graduated from Edgewood High School in 1981. One of his fond memories is the requirement that each student had to sit down with Sister Kathleen to select their classes for the coming year. He recalls that she retired a few years after he graduated.

Sister Mary Marie, OP, known to the family as Sister Pedra, was an elementary teacher for several of the children at Edgewood campus school. She recalls hosting parent conferences when the tall Joe Schmiedicke would bend himself into one of the small chairs in her classroom to hear her comments on a respective offspring's progress.

The selection of an institution for college study was easy, according to David. "The University of Wisconsin was just down the street, a prominent University, and I could live at home and walk to school." Attending the UW was a practical choice, also. David recounted, "I am a practical person, and a shy person. I lived at home and worked to pay for my education myself by working at Methodist Hospital, now Meriter Hospital. I was a housekeeping aide there, and worked every weekend. It was the job I had when Cherie and I first got married, and then we had our first two children. There were good benefits, and it paid pretty well. In total, I worked there for about seven years. It was our core support for awhile. I worked there full-time after graduation."

David graduated from the University in December, 1985, with majors in history and philosophy, two subjects he really had a passion for. "I didn't know what I would do with them," he recalls. The influence of his parents, and the conversations that must have occurred at the family mealtime is evident. He relates that he toyed briefly with majoring in computer science and astrophysics. "I thought about teaching, and took some classes at UW and Edgewood College. I talked with my Dad." However, David's practical side took over once again.

During his final semester in school, David married Cherie Carver in October, 1985. The two had met each other at Madison Area Technical College while singing in a show choir there. David decided that it would take too long to get certified as a teacher. By this time the pressure of raising and providing for a young family was evident for David.

Cherie was a freshman at MATC, and Dave a sophomore at UW when they met. For Cherie, "Teaching was something I was interested in, so I ended up getting an associate degree in Child Development. I've worked with preschoolers since 1985." At the time of this writing, Cherie is employed at Meeting House Nursery School, at the Unitarian Church site. This follows running her own home daycare for 13 years.

Cherie Carver, born on January 30, 1964, was 21 when she and David married. They began their young family immediately, with Peter Schmiedicke born on July 30, 1986, the latest arrival in "the eldest son of an eldest son" in the Schmiedicke tradition. Daughter Laura followed a little over a year later on September 9, 1987. The youngest daughter of Cherie and David, Anna, was born on October 19, 1989.

Dave and Cherie proudly describe their young adult children, Joe's oldest grandchildren. Peter is the most gifted in many respects. Cherie taught him to play guitar. He has a great spatial sense and is a skilled basketball player. Born a sensitive child, Peter at 22, is living at home and works. He has taken coursework at both the University of Wisconsin, Milwaukee, and MATC, entertaining the idea of a major in engineering. Peter is a boy of few words, both patient and shy, a lot like David. He is a cheerleader for his younger sisters, and delighted when they return home from college for vacations. Peter also delights in time spent with Grandfather Joe, especially when he can provide chauffeur services.

Laura at age 21 is a senior at St. Olaf College in Northfield, Minnesota, anticipating graduation in May, 2009, with an English major. Poetry, theater and choir have also been part of her college experience. The most bookish of the three, she read at age two. Laura is most like Cherie, interested in the arts, organized, while introverted like David.

The exact opposite of her older sister, is Anna, at 19 a freshman at Drexel University in Philadelphia, where her Aunt Megan attended college. Anna is reportedly the most 'Schmiedicke,' very smart, extremely athletic, always doing something, overachieving. Currently majoring in biology, she may attend medical school, or pursue engineering. Her grandfather Joe has gone to all her local sporting events through school. Anna is the closest to David, and they enjoy playing sports together.

David traces his work history after he left his work as a hospital maintenance staffer. "I was lucky to get a job with the State of Wisconsin in March of 1988 as a budget analyst, working in the Department of Transportation for two and one half years. Then I went to Department of Administration in the State Budget Office in 1990 and have worked my way up. I became a Team Leader in the Budget Office at age 30 and then was appointed to head the State's Building Program for six months. Since 2001 I have served the State of Wisconsin as Budget Deputy Director and now State Budget Director. I now educate people about programs, creating budgets." Dave's earlier thought of becoming a teacher has a rather non-traditional incarnation in his current position.

Cherie muses on Dave's interest in history and philosophy, and traces it to Joe's influence as the kids were growing up. The house was filled with geography books, maps, Childcraft Books, World Book Encyclopedia, and higher level magazines such as Phi Beta Kappan.

12

MARY SCHMIEDICKE HONG

Fortuna vitrea est **Fortune is glass**

Mary, first daughter in this family that would ultimately welcome four children, was born on February 4, 1965. Joe remembers driving Marian to hospital on a freezing cold Wisconsin winter night, with a temperature of about -20 degrees. He claims that Mary has always hated the cold, and continues to live in a warm climate, and blames it on her cold welcome into the world! Mary Schmiedicke married John Hong, and together they live in Destin, Florida. John is a pilot for Northwest Airlines, and Mary retired from the same airlines after 18 years as a flight attendant, after the birth of the twins. Mary credits her uncle Russell Rajani, now a retired Northwest Airlines pilot, and his influence with her decision to embrace a career with the same airline. She lives the closest to him and had retained close ties with him and his family.

Her twins, Rain Hong and Kai Hong, were born Sept 23, 2006, when their mother was 41. The exciting career as a flight attendant, traveling to exotic destinations, offered an inadequate preparation for motherhood. After the babies were born, Mary's aunts and Joe's sisters, Mary and Nancy, traveled to Florida to help their niece cope with her newly expanded family. Their practical help and the shared family reminiscences renewed the family ties and brought great joy to Mary. Mary spends her spare moments cultivating her creative business, WiredGlass.com. She has developed an incredible line of kiln formed glass mosaics, including night lights and other decorative items, sold online and at art shows.

As Mary describes the growing up years in the Schmiedicke household, she reflects that the family lived in a "bubble," surrounded by the schools of Edgewood, the playground, and a summer pool experience and other outdoor activities. Living just across the street from the Edgewood Campus, Mary recalls that she had calculated the exact number of minutes it required to leave her upstairs bedroom, cross Woodrow St., jump the fence to the campus and be seated in homeroom at Edgewood High School on time for the final morning bell. Of course, being a long-legged athlete, she had an extra advantage.

That "bubble" holding their lives was also circumscribed by regular interaction with the Dominican Sisters of Sinsinawa, who were their teachers at Edgewood preschool, campus school and high school, and colleagues of Joe on the College Faculty. Memories of raiding Sister Mary Rosary's candy jar bring laughs. "We were raised by the nuns, who were part of our everyday life. They baked cakes when we were born, they frequently brought us gifts, they were a part of our First Communion celebrations," Mary recounts.

Mary, encouraged by her mother to apply to the UW, attended school there, and graduated after five years with a BS degree in Interior Design in 1988.

"I decided that my dad was very smart, if he was teaching teachers. The power of that knowledge elevated him up to here," remembers Mary, who continues to be in awe of her dad's accomplishments.

13

LISA SCHMIEDICKE MURE

Fortiter fideliter forsan feliciter
Bravely, faithfully, perhaps successfully

Lisa Schmiedicke Mure, the third child and second daughter of Joe and Marian, was born on June 30, 1966. Her early education mirrored that of her siblings, with attendance at Edgewood Preschool, Kindergarten and elementary grades at Edgewood Campus School, and finally, Edgewood High School. Lisa continued to follow in the family footsteps and graduated from the University of Wisconsin with a BA in Psychology. As the daughter of two teachers, a career in education was an obvious choice. Lisa attended Notre Dame College in Manchester New Hampshire, where she received her Masters in Education.

Subsequently she taught high school for six years before moving into the non-profit world. Lisa has worked in the area of community health and founded a non-profit called Communities for Alcohol and Drug-Free Youth. She is currently a senior consultant at the Community Health Institute, a subsidiary of JSI: a Research and Training group in Boston that boasts public and community health projects around world. Lisa specialized in mental health, health promotion, and disease prevention for adolescents and their families. Lisa currently lives in Holderness, New Hampshire with her girls.

As a divorced single mother of three girls, Lisa proudly describes her daughters. The eldest is Caroline, born May 28, 1996. Caroline is 12, and carries the Schmiedicke athletic genes. She is a golfer and plays basketball; she is also musical, and plays guitar and piano and loves to sing. "Of my daughters, Caroline is least like me and more like her father," Lisa muses. "She is beautiful and likes to be silly, to lip sync. She also is an altar server at our parish."

Ella was born on May 26, 1999. At 9, she is developing into a fine artist, always drawing. In addition to being very bright, Ella always takes care of herself. She has demonstrated that she is inventive, a hard worker and very responsible. This middle daughter plays both soccer and piano, and loves animals.

Maisy, Lisa's youngest, was born July 2, 2002. Six years old and in first grade as of this writing, Lisa reports that she has learned to read and is the funniest kid, with a unique perspective on the world. Maisy loves the outdoors, and the wonderful sports native to her New Hampshire home: sledding, soccer, skiing. Maisy shows signs of being a budding artist, and is also a bit of a worrier and a Mama's girl.

Lisa reflects on growing up so close to Edgewood. "Growing up there was a special, wonderful existence. We had so many layers of family. There was the Schmiedicke family, with so many aunts and uncles, and later, cousins. There was the family of Edgewood, including our dad's colleagues, along with our teachers from Edgewood Campus School and High School. The grand mix of Edgewood cultures included the Sinsinawa Dominicans, so many of our teachers and friends. Beyond those circles was the wider Catholic Community of Madison, including Queen of Peace, Blessed Sacrament and St. Paul's University Chapel. With these many circles around us, each one had its special influence on us. I think of them as layers of insulation that helped to form us and give us confidence." These circles of support and layers of insulation also provided the family, Joe and his children, support in time of crisis. Lisa spoke to the group gathered to honor her dad when the Joseph Schmiedicke Scholarship was created in 2006. Her remarks are included later in this section.

14

MEGAN SCHMIEDICKE FOX

Mater et Magistra **Mother and Teacher**

Megan, the youngest in the family, was born July 21, 1970. She describes the growing up years as a "cocoon experience," with most of the Schmiedicke family experiences revolving around the Edgewood Campus and community. Megan recalls, "I thought everyone had their own cocoon. We walked to school, and came home for lunch." She followed in the footsteps of the three older siblings, and attended Edgewood Preschool, Campus School and Edgewood High School. Another memory is that the family grew up around the Sisters and other things religious. They recall running around the Edgewood Chapel.

Upon graduating, she yearned to go away to a big city, and ultimately decided to attend Drexel University in Philadelphia.

Mary Ellen Gevelinger, O.P.

Reflecting back on the economics of that decision, she thinks that, if she had seriously considered the financial cost involved, she might have chosen to attend Edgewood.

The decision to attend Drexel resulted in graduation with a BS Degree in Finance and Economics. A few years later she returned and obtained a Masters Degree in Management and Information Systems. She worked for 11 years in industry, at a brokerage firm, and for the Federal Reserve, as well as in other banking and consulting positions. She continued to work at some part-time consulting positions until the birth of her fourth child.

Megan is married to Jim Fox, who is the CFO of Dansko, an international footwear company. They have lived in Berwyn, Pennsylvania, a suburb of Philadelphia, for the past six and one half years in a home they recently remodeled. Megan and Jim are the proud parents of four of Joe's grandchildren: Andrew Fox, born November 13, 2002, Christopher Fox, born June 8, 2004, Sarah Fox, born December 16, 2005, and Madeleine Fox, born February 12, 2008. Although they live at a distance, these young grandchildren look forward to two annual trips to the Midwest to visit both Jim's and Megan's families. Megan reports that Grandpa Joe keeps buying video games for the grandchildren. "They're educational, you know," he easily defends his choices.

15

OUR DAD, JOE

Paterfamilias **The Father of the Family**

"Dad left Michigan, his home and family, and set down his roots in Madison, beginning a new life. That provided a model for me to do the same thing," reflected Megan. Indeed, as the youngest of the four, she broke the family practice of attending the local University of Wisconsin in Madison, and left the state to attend Drexel University in Philadelphia. Megan continues, "Now having four kids of my own, I'm amazed at all he did. We were always active as kids, we played football and frisbee; we did a lot of things together."

"He and my mom were the true hippies in the 70's. They had a farm plot, and spent summers planting seeds, growing fruits and vegetables. Dad had a green thumb, and was good at the garden.

Mary Ellen Gevelinger, O.P.

Dad always had one suntanned arm from driving in the car or working in the garden. We ate granola and buckwheat pancakes. There was only one natural foods store on Regent Street, and that's where we shopped."

Joe, born into a family of building contractors, grew up experiencing frequent opportunities to build and remodel and renovate. Those skills helped in the renovation of the house for his mother-in-law, Justina. Where he really demonstrated his capabilities was in the family home, at 812 Woodrow, just across the street from the Edgewood Campus. The family had lived in a few rental properties before Joe and Marian purchased the Woodrow Street property. As the adult children describe it, he totally renovated the family home, from relocating the front door, to adding a full bathroom and bedrooms for everyone upstairs, enlarging the kitchen, and extending the back porch. He is a very good carpenter. In the family basement, he made his own work table. This one example is typical of Joe's many carpentry projects, including helping several of them reroof their homes. The memory of the home remodeling accomplishment is certainly a matter of pride for the family, and contributes to their appreciation that 812 Woodrow continues to be "home" for them, and for Joe and Marsha, Joe's current wife. The children recall at least three other home renovations, carried on under Joe's skillful hand, and intended to be sold for a profit. During these renovations, their own carpentry skills were developed and tested. "Dad is a workhorse, and all four of us got that trait," the girls confess in unison. It is a common theme for the children.

The adult children of Joe Schmiedicke reflect on the changes they've observed in his home community in Michigan. Joe's neighborhood in Grand Rapids was a strong ethnic community with Polish, Germans, Italians, and churches, grocery stores and bakeries catering to those ethnic tastes. It was a tight and friendly community where people could walk everywhere, to church, to school, to the grocery store.

As with many urban areas throughout the country, there was a transformation in the 70's in Grand Rapids. Entire blocks were torn down, new buildings were built and generations of families moved out. Despite all the urban renewal work around there, the home where Joe Schmiedicke grew up, 204 Straight Ave, and his parents' home at 304 Straight Ave, are still owned by family members, at the time of this writing. It was at this latter address that Joe lived with his parents, grandparents, as a baby. Family lore recalls that when Joe was born, the family placed him in a small drawer in place of a bed.

Joe, born into a family that owned a construction company, utilized those building skills in real life and remodeling, and as a metaphor for his life, how he thought about things. David says that Joe always used construction language, and tool analogy. He further traces Joe's interest in technology back to that construction-based upbringing. He recalls his dad referring to technology as "another tool to pull out of the tool box." That metaphor has remained important, with Joe even likening the computer to a hammer as he delivers educational lessons.

Mary Ellen Gevelinger, O.P.

Joe, the carpenter, got a church pew from St. James Church, the parish where he grew up in Grand Rapids. That pew became the kitchen table, and remains so today at 812 Woodrow. He built benches for sitting. And, the kitchen was his domain, as Joe was the parent who did most of the cooking. He is legendary for his pizza and fudge, still favorites with the children and grandchildren.

Lisa describes her dad as social and gregarious; at the same time he can be very private, insulated. He embodies everything that is intelligent and logical, and at the same time wants to put everybody at ease. He is always accommodating where everyone else is, believing that intellect shouldn't be arrogant or snobby. There is no pretense; he is genuine.

When Marian died, the children recall that Joe's mental state was so strong; he was resigned to being the best parent for his four devastated children. They were all involved in many sports. Marian had always been the one attending the games while Joe was at work. Suddenly, he was always there, and drove long distances to cheer them on. Rumor has it that Joe's vocal chords, usually focused on making beautiful music, began to take on the sound of a very loud cheerleader. In recent years, Joe was even banned from a granddaughter's game, when he was too vociferous following a challenged referee's call.

Memories of childhood from the perspective of adulthood and parenthood flooded from the girls. They recalled their dad as the more stern parent, and attribute that to his German Alsace upbringing and family life. On the other hand, the memory of their mom as a more demonstrative and loving parent, due in part to her Italian family life, is very present for them. It fell to Megan, as the youngest, to truly call her dad into being a father. "I was home alone when the older kids had all left home. He was the one who took me shopping and came to my school events." Joe stepped up and became the active and sole parent for his children.

Looking back the children agree that their father grieved in private. He didn't show a lot of emotion, and focused his effort on processing this for children. While he was struggling in his marriage, trying to understand the bouts of depression that consumed Marian, they assume he felt guilt at his inability to find a solution for the problems. As adults, they know that they've given him support and love, as a way of affirming his efforts.

Mary, now a happy and busy parent herself and reflecting on her growing up years, shares an email that she wrote to her dad in November 2008, and Joe's response. The text is presented unedited, in Mary's unique style.

"....Im exhausted with two...I can't imagine four! Kids are huge stresses and so is building a house! I vaguely remember the house on Rahel St???...you were a maverick..there is now an entire network devoted to redoing houses and selling them! And the remodeling you did on 812 woodrow st. I remember the "back porch" and the bath tub on the first floor and the very small bathroom upstairs. How did you get all of that done with 4 little ones running around? I remember helping you nail the roof shingles on the garage. I wanted to use a hammer just as well as you did. I WISH I had you and your knowledge of carpentry now...down here....there are so many little things I want to do to make this house a HOME! I remember the day meg was born. We were down at the Bunge's and you came down to get us and told us we had a new sister. We went home with you and upstairs...Grandma Schmiedicke was there and I remember telling her that Megan was zero years old. I remember exactly where her crib was in the room that used to be where my room was. There are times when I look at Rain...and I think...was I like that when I was two? She's a smart girl...wants to be a big girl sooo bad! She loves to snuggle and I can't get away from her very much...she also has TONS of empathy for a two year old. Im pretty sure I was glued to mom like a bee on a hive. I barely remember instances where I would cry like crazy because I was separated from her. Now that Im a momma, I miss her in a different way because well...it helps having a momma when you gotta BE a momma! Anyway...I loved our times in Grand Rapids with your family. They were adventuresome for us and I loved the change of scenery. I remember the world of Edgewood that we lived in...it was comforting and safe and loving and you were at the core of that. I remember the "power bars" you used to make for me....I call them that now because there was no such thing in the 80's. You would ALWAYS remember to make me a sandwich of banana bread with peanut butter and honey to take "on the road" for my super stardom athletic events. And you always showed up at all of them..even the way out of town ones. I VIVIDLY remember sitting in the back of some bus munching on my sandwiches listening to some hit from the 80's...the sun setting...I was exhausted..but those sandwiches always stayed in my tummy and gave me the fuel I needed to keep going. Thank you for doing that. I KNOW that I have NEVER thanked you for doing that but...It helped me tremendously and I am forever grateful..and I still remember those times today when I'm listening to my 80's songs on the radio...half of them take me back to all the road trips I had as a teen. I remember being in grade school and falling down and hitting my head. They called you over to come and get me. I think you held up a couple of fingers and asked me how many there were. I was so scared...but that made me laugh. I remember being tickled pink one day when you said you'd go fishing with me! I went out to the backyard and dug up worms and got Dave's tackle box and we went down to Lake Wingra and I think I even caught a sunfish. I have wonderful memories Dad. I love you very much. The life you've given me will be very hard to match when it comes to raising my own children. I'm sorry that it's taken me so many years to even realize that...and even more so..to put it to words to you. Meg said it best when we were all in Madison last...It was the night of her birthday and we went out to Cafe Continental for dinner. She said, "You know, in my head, I'm 25, Dad's in his 50's and we're all going to live forever!" So true. I think the exact same way (except I'm always 27). Everything in Madison is frozen in time for me. I could paint a picture of Edgewood 25 years ago exactly how it was...the EXACT place in the fence where we would either CRAWL under the fence to go down to the grade school...and the EXACT place in the fence (slightly bent at the top, directly across the street from our house) where I could jump over it to make it to homeroom before the bell rang at the high school (it took me less than 3 minutes from my bedroom to my homeroom). The mulberry trees at Edgewood...or my fave tree across from our house. It's no longer there...it was my eden. Please know that I love you.. we all do. Kai and Rain look at pictures from this summer and they always say Drappa. They're so cute...and they are proof that miracles do happen. They are the product of a "5% chance" of getting pregnant....and a 30% chance of twins. ..... Thank you for your guidance, your love, your strength, your smarts, your kindness...for the most wonderful life I could have ever asked for! I was not graced with the eloquence of words like my sibs were. But, if I were to paint a picture it would be huge and many shades of red and there would be a plump heart in the center of it. My box of Kleenex is all used up and my shirt is damp from Kai's wet nose."

And her dad's reply.......

"Hi, Mary!

Know first that one's children are the love of one's life --- you know that through the gift of Kai and Rain!

Have no regrets -- the right time is the time you write.

As I near the end of 45 years at Edgewood College and as the life challenge of prostate cancer befriends me, the cascade of memories and experience call me to recognize the many influences on my life formation; the interviewing for my biography reinforces that.

I cannot write the details of that here; others are doing me that service.

In particularly trying times of life, I return to a stanza from a hymn of my youth

> Mother Dear, oh pray for me
>
> Whilst far from heaven and thee;
>
> We travel in a fragile bark
>
> O'er life's tempestuous sea.

It reminds me that we are seldom the directors of our own fate, that our lives intersect with many others -- especially family and friends, and that they are as much our success and sometimes failure as we are; and there are those that watch over us. We are fragile barks; our life travel is on a sea we do not control.

Mary, as the future brings more time, I'll write more. In the meantime, know that it's ok to be 27!

With love, support, and gratitude -------- Dad"

In reflections about their father, the girls continue to remark on his "hippy" qualities, noting that Joe has always been a hoarder. Perhaps this fits with his hobby of stamp collecting, going to antique shops, searching for old post cards and envelopes that carry old stamps.

Having a dad who was a college professor was just an accepted part of family life for the Schmiedicke offspring. "We knew what our dad did as a professor, that he taught teachers. He also directed the summer session at Edgewood College for many years."

It is daughter-in-law Cherie who summarizes Joe's legacy, coming from a strong blue collar background, balanced with huge intellect. These two complementary aspects of his life go hand in hand. She also comments that Joe does not possess a huge ego, and while basically shy, is a bit of a performer. Joe has a beautiful singing voice, and has performed in some Gilbert and Sullivan Operettas. Son Dave is like his dad, both shy, and at the same time able to perform in front of a group, having learned to overcome his innate shyness. With his inherited height, David is a recognizable physical presence.

The family home at 812 Woodrow Street is very significant in the life of the family through the years. It is the only home the adult children truly remember, and it is the heart of the family for the grandchildren. David reminisces, "We all grew up there, and our kids grew up there. We have great memories and not so great, in fact, heavy memories. It was significant that as a family, we chose to continue to live there after our mom died. We moved there in 1970." There was a new baby, the house remodeling project was underway, and Joe was completing his PhD at the University of Wisconsin. The residence at 812 Woodrow Street remains the family home in 2009. Joe had a vision of how the house should be and reconfigured the house to conform to that vision. Physical work provided an outlet for him and offered some needed balance in his life. Although he was not a sports or fitness guy Joe made the entire house new, creating a new kitchen, refashioning the upstairs by adding bedrooms and a new bathroom. There was a new deck on back of the house, and the front door was relocated. The home hold the family memories of times spent together, times being kids and adults.

Lisa prepared some remarks for the ceremony establishing the Joseph E. Schmiedicke Future Teachers' Award at Edgewood, and shares them here:

"Good afternoon. My name is Lisa Schmiedicke Mure and I am Dr. Joe's third child. I should probably let you all know that our family NEVER called my dad, Dr. Joe. We have always known that to be a term of endearment for his students and colleagues here at Edgewood.

"As some of you may know, Edgewood has been our family's extended family since we were born, living just up the drive on Woodrow Street for most of our lives. We went to nursery school at Edgewood, to kindergarten (two years!) at Edgewood, and to high school at Edgewood. By the time we were each ready for college, Edgewood was the LAST place we wanted to be…so take no offense that I am, I think, the only one of Dr. Joe's children to have actually taken a class here—a winterim course on the origins of patriarchy in Mesopotamia—and it was a fascinating, compelling and wonderful class! AND, it helped me get my University of Wisconsin diploma a semester early!

"But for most of our lives, Edgewood College was not an educational institution in its traditional sense. It was our second home, a second family, a second sense of the world. We visited Sinsinawa Dominicans in their offices as children, stealing their candy. We played pool in the student lounge, we photocopied our handprints in the mailroom at Regina Hall. We went to the Mound for spaghetti dinners and fell in love with their famous "Nun's Bread" (what we dubbed it, anyway).

"The Sisters remembered our birthdays, taught us piano, told stories of their missionary trips abroad, explored botany with us on walks in the woods, and always, always greeted us with warm hearts and broad smiles. They were and still are the best people I have known—Sister Miriam, Sister Marie Stephen, Sister Nancy Grace (sic), and so many more.

"And what I remember of my father during our years in the Edgewood circle is a montage of sorts: his trips all over the country for NCATE accreditations, his love of teaching, his long-standing friendship with faculty and students alike, and, of course, Phil from the dining hall who still makes sure we are well stocked with his Christmas cookies each year.

"My father is from the generation who are never seen in shorts, without a collared shirt or belt, who rarely if ever wears sneakers, who used to speak Latin at our dinner table just to see us roll our eyes, and then his blue eyes would twinkle. He has kept us up-to-date on new presidents and faculty, those retiring or who have passed away – always wanting us to know how our second family is doing in our long absences.

"But I think, too, that my father is a private man. He chooses quiet ways to show and feel pride in us, subtle ways to express emotion, discreet ways to lend a hand and show support. Like his father before him, he helps us all with construction projects small and large, replacing windows, sagging porches, and then, of course, thinks he can reroof his own house! He helped rebuild my kitchen one year, visited my sister after her baby was born, showed off my sister's website, and was always beaming when talking of my brother's big promotions.

"His pride is even greater when it comes to his grandchildren, and there are twelve now. And we are so grateful that he has such a presence in their lives – sending them pictures and notes. And, has anyone seen him attend a sporting event of his child's or grandchild's? Well, I thought the pattern would end once my siblings and I left high school and college."

16

OUR SCHMIEDICKE GRANDPARENTS

Maximus in minimis **Great in little things**

    The four oldest grandchildren in the larger Schmiedicke family are quick to remark on the profound influence of "very incredible grandparents," who had a strong influence on their dad and on them as well. Lisa described them as generous, giving, and faithful with a grandfather who got up at 4:00 am and picked up day old bakery goods to take to the local soup kitchen. This same grandfather would invite his grandchildren, when they were present, to help him make holiday bags to take to the soup kitchen for distribution to the poor of Grand Rapids.

The Schmiedicke Grandparents were very significant to David, as the eldest son of Joe, their eldest son, and more importantly, the first grandchild in the family. Trips to see the grandparents in Michigan, and extended summer visits to spend time with them are favorite memories for all of Joe's children. The girls now reflect that these longer summer visits were directly related to Marian's bouts of depression. David and Cherie recall taking their youngest children, as the first great-grandchildren, for an annual Michigan trip to visit the older generation.

"My grandfather was one of the smartest guys, not in the sense of being highly educated, but in construction skills and ability," recalls David. He recounts the story of "Grandpa Ed's" remarkable intervention to save the local family parish church of St. James in Grand Rapids, Michigan. The story is told that the church was settling into the ground and was predicted to collapse, according to experts. Engineers, called in to consult, reported back that the parishioners would have to abandon the church, as there was no viable solution. Ed Schmiedicke, lifelong parishioner and owner of his own construction company, had a better idea. He jacked up the entire church structure and poured a new concrete foundation under it. The church didn't fall down as predicted, and still stands today. David recalls hearing his dad, Joe, proudly tell this story.

All the grandchildren agree that their grandmother, Madeline Schmiedicke, was a wonderful person, so loving and compassionate. David remembers that, although she was busy with her own large family, she always wanted to listen to us and to offer suggestions. As the oldest of some 40 grandchildren, David was just a few years younger than his Dad's youngest siblings. Most of the Schmiedicke family lived close by, and most remain in Michigan today. The Wisconsin grandchildren visited Grand Rapids just once or twice a year, wrapped in the loving arms of so many aunts and uncles. Their dad's youngest sister, Ruth, was just 6 years older than David. The big family events and reunions were always eagerly anticipated by David and his sisters. The visits to their grandmother were especially comforting.

All the grandchildren are quick to remark that their Schmiedicke grandparents were very religious people, frequently attending daily Mass. Their Grandmother had many rosaries, and was always fingering one of them, reflective of deep devotion to the Blessed Mother.

Lisa's recollection of her grandmother is that she was calm, patient, kind. "She had 47 grandchildren and yet each of us felt like we were her special one. She remembered our birthdays. Our family believes that a miracle occurred when she died." In true old-time style, there was a three day wake with five visitation times. Lisa arrived on the last day with Caroline, who was about six months old. "Our aunt Linda, dad's sister and the "mother" of her siblings, stood up and told this story. She and her sisters selected a dress for their mother to wear in the casket, a blue dress with white flowers. The rosary they selected from their mother's many rosaries was a crystal one, to match the white flowers in her dress. When we came in the final day to close the casket, the white beads had turned golden, a soft shade of yellow. Another aunt, very outspoken, declared that she was there: 'those beads were white and now they're gold.' It was certainly a sign of the presence of Mother Mary, and a sign of favor for their grandmother and her family."

David recalls a large celebration for their grandparents' 45th Wedding Anniversary, that included a framed proclamation of congratulations and blessing from the Pope. Chronic medical conditions made it seem impossible that they would live to celebrate their 50th together. Coming from hardy stock, they lived until nearly 55 years of married life.

The girls reflected on the roots in their lives. "Our grandparents lived in the same house all their lives; our father lives in same house we grew up in. After our mother died there was a big question whether we, Dad and us kids, would remain in the house." According to the girls, their brother wasn't sure, but they wanted to stay so the family did. Today, that home on Woodrow St. in Madison still holds much significance and many memories for the family.

17

OUR MOTHER, MARIAN

Materfamilias **Mother of the family**

David reminisces, "Our Mother, Marian Rajani, was born in Chicago in 1940. Justina was her mother and our grandmother. We didn't know Angelo, her Italian-born father, who died while she was in high school. I think he was an engineer with the City of Chicago and built bridges. Her brother, our Uncle Russell, is a retired pilot."

Grandmother Rajani lived in Madison for many years. Cherie recalls, "She spent time with us and our oldest 2 children when they were young." She moved to Atlanta in the early 90's to be near her son, Russ. Grandmother Justina Rajani passed away in April 2008. Her grandchildren, Lisa and David, attended the memorial service for her in Chicago in September, 2008.

Marian's father died suddenly, when she was in her teens. This caused the family great sadness, as well as financial struggles. Her mother, Justina, had a hard time with his death. David, the oldest, recalls there was a question of whether her father was a legal immigrant and subsequent questions of whether there would be social security benefits for the family.

Marian left Chicago and went to Marquette University in Milwaukee, perhaps in a desire to leave behind the sad memories of losing her father. Besides her mother, her family included her brother Russell Rajani. As of this writing, Russell lives in Sanoia, Georgia, where he owns a horse farm. Russell is a retired navy fighter pilot, and was employed as an airline pilot with Republic Airlines and Northwest Airlines, prior to his retirement. Although they haven't lived very close to their uncle, his nephew and nieces recall admiring his lifestyle, and a flashy red sports car that he drove.

The girls remember their mom as so funny, and not caring what anybody thought; she was bit of a fashion queen, wearing gauchos before they were in fashion, and doing yoga when no one else did. They recall Marian, walking up and down Woodrow Street, doing exercises. Even more importantly, Marian was the one who provided opportunities and encouraged them to try sewing class, violin, softball, to learn and develop their own talents.

Lisa has a fond memory that she wanted to quit band where she played the clarinet. "Mom cried for months, because she really wanted me to persevere. I ultimately did quit." Lisa also recalls that Marian was extremely loving, always telling her and her siblings, "I love you; you're beautiful." She possessed both a sensitivity and a sense of whimsy. "I try to be that way for my kids," Lisa muses.

One of Joe's early remodeling projects was for Justina, Marian's mother. David's memory is that the family bought a house on the east side, intended to be a home for Justina, who had moved to Madison from Chicago. "I helped him renovate it and remember blowing insulation into the attic. Dad gutted the kitchen. The year was 1977. When it was complete, she didn't want to live in the house; she was a challenging individual. Perhaps there was some mental illness that we didn't understand."

Each of the four Schmiedicke children recalled their mother, Marian, in deeply emotional terms. Marian died on May 16, 1983. As of this writing, she has been gone for over 25 years, gone for more years than any of her children experienced her loving presence. She and Joe had not yet celebrated their 21st wedding anniversary. David was almost 20 years old, Mary had turned 18 in February, and was weeks away from graduation from Edgewood High School. Lisa was 16 at the time, and Megan, the youngest in the family, was 12.

David is adamant that he wants to separate the way she died from the positive things she accomplished in her life. He tells the story of her final day. "I was finishing final exams at the University of Wisconsin, my sophomore year. I was the last one to see her alive, and I was the one who found her after she had taken her own life. My dad, Megan and I were at home. Mary and Lisa were at the library downtown. I was the one who had to tell my sisters, and take them to my grandmother, Justina, and tell her. It was a very tough situation. I kept wondering why, and did I have some responsibility for her death?"

David continues his reflections about his mother. "My mom and I were very close, and she confided in me quite a bit. I could talk to her. I was hearing a lot of things I couldn't handle. She was always trying to overcome her own struggles and wanting advice. My mom and dad struggled in their marriage. They married very young and were inexperienced. Mom struggled with mental illness and she and dad sought some help." Although there was a stigma attached to mental illness in the 1970's and 1980's, Madison was on the cutting edge as far as treatment was concerned. The family recalls that Marian was really struggling her last Christmas for the family. There were barely any gifts under the Christmas tree, and no presents for David. Cherie insightfully remarks that as the oldest in the family, Dave saw Marian and Joe's loving relationship and their struggles, perhaps more closely than the younger girls.

The girls recall that Marian's death was announced at Edgewood very publicly, since the family was so well known at all three schools. The response of the Edgewood community was outstanding, and is still fresh in the mind of the family. Joe recalls that Sister Joan Leonard, his colleague at the College, was the first of many sisters to arrive at the family home, to offer comfort and support. Lisa recalls the huge outpouring of support from the St. Paul's University Chapel Community, where the family worshipped. Marian cooked chili for the soup kitchen there, and

Joe and Marian had developed the Faith Formation Program for high school students in the parish. In Lisa's memory, the funeral at St. Paul's was huge, with standing room only in the Church. Joe courageously addressed the congregation. Although in the Catholic tradition earlier there had been discrimination against a Catholic funeral for a suicide victim, the girls recall no such discrimination at Marian's death, only support and outreach. Food, comfort, and prayer surrounded Joe and his children. Lisa concludes, "I was 16; I didn't feel anything negative. Her funeral was a tribute to who she was: loving, giving. She gave a lot to others, and didn't take in return. As much as we had to survive tragedy, there were so many layers of support for us." The entire family recalls there was an outpouring of comfort in their tragedy.

The family also recalls the support of the school and the sensitivity of teachers. Megan was helped quite a bit, being only 12, and still in grade school. In high school they had sessions with a school grief counselor and could talk through their pain with a support group. At the time of Marian's death, Mary was graduating from high school in a few weeks, and Lisa was just a year behind.

When David was a freshman at the UW, he contracted mononucleosis and had to miss school. Marian interceded for him with his teachers, and brought his work home to him so that he wouldn't fail his courses. His mom's connection to the University, and the many friends she had made there, extended assistance to David, even following her death. He was allowed to take his final exams much later, due to the influence of Marian's friends at the University of Wisconsin, where she worked. David recalls that he struggled the two semesters following his mother's death, in fall and spring, trying to come to some understanding of his mother's choices.

Megan, closely resembling her mother, quietly remembers her mom as relatively quiet with a soft voice and very nurturing. Mary, now a mother of twins herself, recalls Marian as a wonderful mom, very loving, very giving, someone who took in any loser. Her memories are around the transition from high school to college, and her mother's influence. "I was 18 when she died; it was the week before my high school graduation. I was a wimp and didn't know where I wanted to go to school. She had encouraged me to apply to University of Wisconsin. That is where I ended up going. She was very down to earth. I was in a daze at my graduation."

Marian's daughters shared many collective memories of their mom. Clearly, in their minds, she was a hippie. She sewed her daughters' clothes as well as her own clothes. She frequently wore gauchos, much to their embarrassment. They recall a "gorgeous purple dress" she made for one of them, she painted on fabric and practiced yoga before it was fashionable. While she had a huge heart, and compassion for the underdog, she was not a good cook.

They reflected that their mom wanted them to experience a lot of things. They were initiated into the arts, took classes through the Community Recreation Department, and experienced music lessons. Each of the four played piano or sang in a chorus. Sports were part of each of their lives. She invited them to feel positive about themselves. She kept asking them, "Who are you going to be? How are you going to live your life?" She was thinking about them, too. She was committed to us kids, very passionate, present at every game and recital.

Characteristic of women of her generation, Marian was very involved in liberalization of church in the 1960's, influenced by the women's movement of the day. She and Joe became involved at St. Paul's University Chapel, at the request of Monsignor McMurrough, then pastor of St. Paul's. Together, they developed and ran the religious education program for high school youth for some years. She took her children to church and Sunday School afterwards. According to her daughters, it was St. Paul's and the energetic spirit of Church they found there, that was life-giving for Joe and Marian. Their closest friends worshipped there and shared a common vision of Church.

Marian was equally devoted to her Bible Study group with a group of neighborhood mothers through Blessed Sacrament Parish. In those years, the '70's and early '80's, many American Catholics in the enthusiasm of the Post Vatican II Church, found the freedom to deepen their personal Journey with God. Marian, and so many others, began to step out of the traditional roles for women, and engaged in theological and spiritual exploration at their parishes, and in small groups, gathering to study scripture or simply to gather in prayerful support.

Her daughters characterize Marian as a woman with a deep spiritual interest, something she has clearly passed on to her children. She often addressed her offspring as "Children of God," they fondly recall.

"Mother battled post-partum depression after two pregnancies at least," according to Lisa. "It was a quiet thing, and we'd go to Michigan for a few weeks or months to stay with our aunts and uncles." Marian felt she was heading toward another serious depression and had sought professional help. In the 1980's medical intervention for depression and mental illness was still in the developmental stages. Lisa concluded that her mother's faith was remarkable, and she felt like her life was so painful that dying was going to bring her to God.

Megan humorously tells that her mother was the parent who accepted responsibility for seeing that the children received the sacraments and had the proper preparation. When Marian died, Megan, just 12, was not old enough to have been confirmed. Clearly overwhelmed by the demands of his family and work, Joe paid no attention to that fact. Megan didn't know what to do. When it came time for her to be married, and the priest asked for her sacramental records, Megan owned up to the missing sacrament. The priest invited her to participate in the upcoming confirmation ceremony in the parish, and finally Megan was confirmed!

The girls further reflected on the things that they miss, not having their mother in their adult life. "I wish I could ask her about that day I was born." "I want to thank her for raising us, for the sacrifices she and dad made for us." "I want to give her more credit for her life." "I wish I could talk to her as an adult."

"I'd love for her to see my kids, and to remember her laughing at us when we were little." "I'd like to hear her call him 'Daddy Joe' again."

As her children were older and everyone was in school, Marian went to work at the University of Wisconsin, in the late 1970's. She joined a group of women in the Statewide ECG Computer Service. The women received electrocardiograms via fax from around the State of Wisconsin, tests that were read by Dr. Richard Wasserburger.

On the 20th anniversary of her death, daughter-in-law Cherie Schmiedicke assembled a booklet of tributes to Marian. Many letters came from her co-workers at the UW, as well as parishioners from St. Paul's and Blessed Sacrament. The sentiment in these letters was similar, recalling a good friend, fun-loving co-worker, and joyful, faith-filled woman.

18

MARSHA CALLAHAN

Deo Gratias **Thank God**

Joe Schmiedicke and Marsha Callahan were married on September 26, 2007. But Marsha was a part of the Schmiedicke family long before that time. Marsha was born in Illinois, with two brothers and one sister in her family. She attended school at St. Mary's in Dixon, staffed by the Dominican Sisters of Sinsinawa. There is probably a direct link from that influence, predicting that Marsha would go on to attend Edgewood College. Even after graduating, with a major in English, Marsha remained at the College, working in a variety of positions including the Office of Special Projects and managing the College Bookstore. As of this writing, she has been employed at the University of Wisconsin Foundation as a Development Assistant for the past five years. Marsha's hobbies include needlework and reading. For her part, Marsha treasures the relationship with Joe's children and grandchildren. She has nurtured special relationships with David and Cherie's three children, because they lived close by, and as a family they all celebrated birthdays and holidays.

When asked about their relationship with Marsha, and her influence on the family, there is a unanimous chorus of "Thank God for Marsha," The girls even go so far as to claim that sometimes their Dad was the "barking order" type, whereas Marsha is a great go-between. All four family members acknowledge the difficult place she assumed, coming into a family with four grown children, not the mother of any of them. Daughter-in-law Cherie values the relationship Marsha has fostered with grandchildren. When David and Cherie's children were young, they referred to the older generation with a one word name, "GrandpaMarsha."

Furthermore, there is a sense that Marsha has been a wonderful companion to their dad. When a spouse dies, there is a sadness and a loneliness, an empty space that children cannot and should not be expected to fill. While they view their dad as a very private person, dealing quietly with the sadness in his life, Marsha is recognized as the confidant for him.

Each of the four siblings echoes gratitude for her presence. They agree that Marsha brings Joe connection, and comfort now in his illness. He has someone to take care of him, someone to listen to him. She keeps him from becoming isolated, in quiet ways.

Marsha invited him to be a different person, according to Cherie, a consummately patient person. While he was often busy at work when his own children were younger, it has been different with his grandchildren. He has become more intentional about what he wanted to pass on to them. With Joe, it is frequently educational and technology based: he will send them an article, buy them software, make sure that they have updated computers. He has succeeded in opening up a new world for them through his own interest in technology. "That's how he tells you he loves you."

Cherie concludes, "With Marsha's influence, I've watched him grow up, emotionally. He wanted me to call him Joe, but I choose to call him Dad." While Mary, Lisa and Megan have been separated geographically from Madison, it is Joe and Marsha, Dave and Cherie, along with their family of Peter, Laura and Anna, who have become a family. While Joe and Marsha don't have children, "our kids are their children," reflects Cherie. They host Thanksgiving and Christmas, and both are excellent cooks.

David and Cherie reflect on the good partnership between Joe and Marsha. These fine chefs enjoy trying new recipes, doing things together, traveling to different places. Marsha might take in a stitchery show while Joe is off prowling through antique shops to augment his stamp collection.

In the family circle, Marsha has never tried to fill the void left by the death of their mother, the children agree. Marsha is caregiver and she has done it so beautifully. At this stage in their relationship, they are moving from partnership to dependency.

Mary Ellen Gevelinger, O.P.

Through this transition as Joe's illness diminishes him, she has done such a beautiful job in acceptance. She has experienced it all: anger, depression, dealing with it with humor and grace. It has been so tough for her. Marsha tries to maintain Joe's dignity.

19

JOE'S LEGACY—IN DAVID'S WORDS

Filioque **And from the son**

"The Legacy of Joe Schmiedicke, my dad, is that of a life long learner and a builder. He has built a program from scratch at Edgewood College and that program was always well respected throughout the State. He has produced teachers who convey that ethic of learning in schools throughout the State.

"He had a vision of how the population was changing and responded to that, just how a building has to change to meet new needs. The metaphor of a builder is significant here. He created the weekend college, developed the summer session with some significant programs. He realized that graduate programs were a practicality for a small college to survive. He was good at finding niches and filling them. A small college can be nimble and respond to different demographics and needs quickly. That's his professional side.

"On the personal side, the title of builder is certainly fitting. There was the total renovation of the house on Woodrow and other home renovation projects. The builder had to adapt to the available materials and do the best that he could with them. He has always considered the practicality of things, how to do things better. He has an ego. Grandpa Ed used to say, 'Joe always thinks he's right.' Dad has learned how to make room for other perspectives. He is a builder who has a passion and love for what he is building, and he has infused that into the college, home and family: that's his legacy.

"He set a foundation for the future and is seeing the horizon now. There is so much past that horizon that he's built, relationships with children and grandchildren and all people he's touched."

FAMILY PHOTOS

Adult Schmiedicke Children, Christmas, 2007

Mary Schmiedicke Hong holding Rain Hong with husband
John Hong holding Kai Hong

Lisa Schmiedicke Mure holding Maisy; l to r:
daughters Caroline and Ella

David and Cherie Schmiedicke, with children, l to r:
Laura, Peter and Anna

L to r: The Fox Family: Andrew, John holding daughter Madeleine, Megan Schmiedicke Fox, Sarah, and Christopher

September 26, 2007 wedding of Marsha Callahan and Joe Schmiedicke. Witnesses are David and Cherie Schmiedicke

All Its Life

All its life
the grizzled cedar
has stood
strong against the wind
assaulted in its youth
its prime
its ageless years

only its hardiest branches
remain
to present themselves to the autumn light
the beauty of their particularity
unrecognized by the unseasoned eye.

Pruned over years of
rhythmic growth --
Mother Nature
Sister Nature
Brother Nature
Father Nature
hard at work --
the tree is perfect
in its misshapen shapeliness,
become what it alone could be
a blessed nature
obedient and responsive
grateful and receptive
a grace to this lakeside hummock.

In the end
it tells me
this truth remains:
if one lives in high wind
one expects to be shaped by it.

-- Marianne Novak Houston
Autumn, 2003

All Its Life by Marianne Novak Houston
Graphic Tree Overlay Produced by Caroline Mure, Granddaughter, Holderness NH
Gifted to Joseph E. Schmiedicke, PhD; Edgewood College; Dean, School of Education
On the Occasion of His Seventieth Birthday January 31, 2008
By Rebecca Zambrano, CTELL Project Coordinator; A TESOL Project Sited at Edgewood College
Under the Direction of Joseph E. Schmiedicke, PhD; Funded by the United States Department of Education

III

EDGEWOOD FAMILY 1963-2009

20

EDGEWOOD COLLEGE

Initio In the beginning

Edgewood College joins with Edgewood Campus School and Edgewood High School, to form the collective Schools of Edgewood, founded and now sponsored by the Sinsinawa Dominican Sisters. The schools are located on the 55 acre property bordered by Monroe Street on the Northwest, and adjacent to Lake Wingra on the East. These three schools of Edgewood trace their beginning to St. Regina Academy, opened by the sisters in 1861, on a location in downtown Madison near the property that would be the site of St. Raphael's Cathedral, and two blocks from the Capital. St. Regina was the only Catholic Academy in Madison at the time, and gives the Schools of Edgewood their place as the oldest sponsored schools of the Sinsinawa Dominicans still in existence.[5]

The move to the present site of the Schools of Edgewood was predicated by a gift of the property to the Dominican Sisters by Cadwallader Washburn in 1881. Washburn served as Governor of the State of Wisconsin from 1872-1873. Edgewood was home to him and his family, and boasted gardens, orchards, and farm animals. His gift, with the stipulation that the property be used "for educational purposes," was spurned by the City of Madison, the University of Wisconsin, and the State of Wisconsin. The Dominican Sisters were delighted to accept the property and moved St. Regina Academy to the new site for the beginning of fall classes in 1881. Eventually the school assumed the "Edgewood" name.

With the move to the new site, St. Regina Academy became Edgewood Academy. The development of the Mission of Edgewood academy mirrored the development of educational opportunities for women in the Upper Midwest. Edgewood College officially opened as a Junior College for women in September of 1927. The new College joined Edgewood High School to enjoy space in a beautiful new structure, opened in February, 1927. That building, designed by noted Philadelphia architect Albert Kelsey, grandson of Governor Washburn, continues as the site of Edgewood High School.[6]

Growth in the College was slow, tempered by the effects of the depression. Finally, a full four year College emerged in 1940. While the two year program had offered an Associate of Arts

Degree, the four year program had a new focus. The purpose, as expressed in the college catalog for 1941-1942, defined the new direction, *"to prepare qualified teachers for Art, Kindergarten-Primary and elementary schools and for Commerce in secondary schools."*[7] The Sinsinawa Dominicans, dedicated to the ministry of education, viewed the four year college as a place for education of their young members, as well as for young lay women pursuing a career in education.

From this humble beginning, Edgewood College has grown and expanded with new academic facilities and residence halls, into multiple schools, departments, degrees and programs, both in the Liberal Arts and Sciences as well as Professional Preparation Programs.

In the early days of the College, various sisters were named president, a title they assumed along with a variety of other duties. Thus, most of the responsibility for the fledgling institution was assumed by the Dean of the College. Finally, in 1950, Sister Nona McGreal, OP was appointed as the first full-time President of Edgewood College. The 18 years of her tenure, until 1968, were filled with growth and expansion at the college, due to support from the Dominican Congregation, and the vision and energy of Sister Nona.

Sister Nona, in an interview in 2008 for this biography, recalled the challenges and struggles of those early days. "You know, we started as a team and the lay men and women who joined the sisters, caught the spirit. We had no building for college in those days. I was given a little money, and 14 acres, so we decided that the only thing we could do with that much money was (to build) a Campus School. That would get us going. The elementary students were attending classes in the convent building. If we moved students out of the convent, it freed up room for the college. So, it was a double play."

Sister Nona's memory of Joe's arrival at Edgewood is still clear. "He was among the first of the lay people I hired. I well remember I was at the side door watching for him and his wife, and they drove up in a little red car....if it wasn't just after he graduated from Marquette, it was shortly after. I knew immediately that he was one of the gifts we had at Edgewood. I remember his enthusiasm, his way with people, his excellence as a faculty member, the contributions he made as a faculty member and his excellence as a teacher."

Dr. Schmiedicke's memory of the event mirrors Sister Nona's. "I remember driving up to the side door of Edgewood College in my little red car, with my wife and our new baby son beside me. Sister Nona was at the door to meet us. Actually, my advisor at Marquette had sent me a note from a ripped lunch bag, with a name and phone number on it, telling me about a little college in Madison, looking for a professor to teach education. The rest is history."

These memories chronicle what was a rather inauspicious beginning, in 1963, for this newly minted MEd from Marquette University, in what would become an outstanding career in education, with an influence far beyond the walls of Marquette or

Edgewood. Why Marquette? Why Edgewood? Why Madison? Why Sister Nona? Coincidence? Providence?

The memories and tributes in the upcoming chapters come from taped interviews and written tributes, submitted by colleagues, alumnae and friends in 2008 and 2009, for inclusion in this biography.

21

SINSINAWA DOMINICAN SPONSORSHIP

Ex abundantia cordis, os loquitur **From the abundance of the heart, the mouth speaks.**

"The Sinsinawa Dominican values flow from the Gospel, providing a focus for every educational ministry sponsored by the Sinsinawa Dominicans." [8]

In the 1980's, the Sinsinawa Dominican Office of Sponsorship engaged in a process with the schools sponsored by the Order to articulate the common values that support the ministry of education in the sponsored schools. In the document entitled "At the Heart of Ministry is Relationship," the Dominican Values were defined for all the schools. The values include Truth,

Compassion, Justice, Community, and Partnership. The five values, hallmarks of all Sinsinawa Dominican sponsored schools, wave proudly on banners adorning the Edgewood Campus. The values also are embedded in every aspect of life at the College.

In 2009, the Edgewood College Mission summarizes these values:

Edgewood College, rooted in the Dominican tradition, engages students within a community of learners committed to building a just and compassionate world. The College educates students for meaningful personal and professional lives of ethical leadership, service and a lifelong search for truth.[9]

As this biography was moving toward completion, Cohort VII of the Doctoral Program in Educational Leadership, a legacy of Dr. Joe's incredible vision, reflected that the Dominican Values are truly the recipe that shaped his life and professional accomplishments. A brief description of the values, as outlined in that 1980's document, gives insight into the unfolding trajectory of his professional life at Edgewood College and beyond.

Truth: That which conforms to reality or fact

- We study and pray to discover truth.
- We acknowledge those prejudices and social conditions that keep us from the truth.
- We foster the arts and sciences as means to reveal truth.

- We speak the truth, accepting its consequences and confirming our belief that truth sets God's power free.

Compassion: Mercy and empathy with another's suffering

- We recognize the intrinsic dignity and interdependence of all creation.
- We acknowledge local issues, sources of injustice and sorrow that make heavy burdens for the people.
- We support and cooperate with each person's efforts to become his/her own best self.

Justice: Behavior that recognizes the rights and responsibilities of all God's creation

- We interact with others with integrity.
- We work to assure the rights of all people, especially women and children.
- We commit our energies to issues of poverty and racism.
- We pay just salaries and provide just procedures to hear the concerns of those with whom we minister.

Community: A manner of relating based on our recognition of the interdependence of all nature

- We nurture relationships which enhance the well being of persons, the earth, and all beings.
- We communicate honestly, openly.
- We value cooperation over competition.

Partnership: A mutual relationship of mature persons who recognize their shared call to actions of justice and love.

- We foster unity in mission that strengthens local leadership and enables the creative, innovative development of gifts for the sake of God's people.
- We practice participative decision-making. [10]

22

DR. JOE, GOURMET CHEF

Contemplare contemplata allis tradere

To reflect and share with others the fruits of your reflection

A little known fact about Dr. Joe is that he is a gourmet chef. The earliest mention of this is a memory from his daughter Mary, who recalls the wonderful peanut butter and honey sandwiches her dad made and sent along with her on trips to athletic games. Those sandwiches carried nourishment for both body and spirit, providing energy and encouragement for the competition.

A carefully guarded family recipe is coming to light in this biography. You, the reader, can now attempt to replicate Dr. Joe's famous fudge recipe.

THE SECRET SCHMIEDICKE FABULOUS FUDGE RECIPE

Ingredients:

2.5 cups of sugar [1.5 cups of super granulated; 1 cup of regular granulated]

.75 cup [1.5 sticks] butter or margarine.

1 - 5 oz. can evaporated milk.

1.5 - 12 oz. packages semi-sweet chocolate chips [Valrona or Scharffen Berger] or 18 oz. of broken chunk chocolate [Valrona or Scharffen Berger] or, if you are in Madison WI, James J. Chocolate on Monroe Street.

1-7 oz. jar of Marshmallow Creme.

To Taste: 1 cup of chopped nuts of choice or none at all
            1 teaspoon of vanilla or none at all.

Preparation:

On a cookie sheet, lay out a sheet of parchment.

In a large heavy saucepan on medium heat, place the sugar, butter, and evaporated milk.

Bring contents to full rolling boil on the medium heat; stir constantly.

When contents reach 234 degrees on a candy thermometer, remove from heat.

Immediately add chocolate and marshmallow; stir until completely melted. Immediately add vanilla and nuts if desired; stir to mix well.

Pour mixture on parchment and spread to desired thickness.

Lightly score fudge into one-inch squares; let cool for about four hours.

Break fudge at scores. [11]

≈≈≈≈≈≈

Just as Joe the cook, nourished his family and continues that history by cooking for his grandchildren, so Joe, the leader, has cooked up a mix consisting of the Dominican values, personal vision and wisdom, mixing those who sit at the table, and adding his own spice and inspiration. The result is the

RECIPE FOR

JOSEPH E. SCHMIEDICKE'S 46 YEAR TENURE AT EDGEWOOD COLLEGE

A recipe is a framework for a specific outcome, usually a food item to provide nourishment for the human body. Feeding others is a basic necessity for human life, and the early and primary responsibility of parents. Feeding others is also one of the Works of Mercy in the Catholic tradition, articulated as *Feeding the Hungry*. Gathering around food, celebrating a meal together is frequently the gathering medium for friends and family, celebrations of birth, marriage and death, and a way to build community. Comfort foods have a special way of reminding persons of how one's family celebrated events and holidays, what they enjoyed eating together. Nourishing the body is a way of serving others, seeing that they have what they need for life's journey, enjoying the delight a person has in eating the food so lovingly prepared.

While the opportunity to feed others is important to one's sense of pleasure and fulfillment, the parallel experience of being fed by another is significant in other ways. Realizing that one is held in esteem and value contributes to the encounter of sharing the food.

Nourishing of mind and spirit of one's companions on the journey is equally a daunting task and a satisfying experience. During his 46 years at Edgewood College, there have been myriad opportunities for Joe Schmiedicke to engage in such nourishing, and to be nourished in return. Examining the years as they unfolded raises many questions about the ingredients in the recipe. What was the basis of the nourishing that occurred at Edgewood College? What values provided the foundation? What spirit inspired the exchanges that created dynamic growth?

The chapters that follow define the Edgewood College Dominican Values as Dr. Schmiedicke has lived them. The accounts from faculty, staff, friends and alums come from interviews and comments solicited for this biography in 2008 and 2009.

23

TRUTH

Veritas **Dominican Motto**

Truth: That which conforms to reality or fact
- We study and pray to discover truth.
- We acknowledge those prejudices and social conditions that keep us from the truth.
- We foster the arts and sciences as means to reveal truth.
- We speak the truth, accepting its consequences and confirming our belief that truth sets God's power free.

The Edgewood College value of truth is an obvious place to begin to chronicle Joe Schmiedicke's 46 year tenure at the College.

Dr. Joe: A Lifetime of Service

He is considered by Sam Barosko, a retired professor who shared an office with Joe for 21 years, to be "the most outstanding scholar I have ever known. Joe shared with me his extensive knowledge of classical studies. He appreciated my interest in history and was responsible for encouraging me to pursue in-depth studies of the Church and medieval history."

Joe's own resume chronicles his deep educational experience. It includes

- B.A. 1959 Catholic University of America, Philosophy, English, Classical Languages
- M.Ed. 1962 Marquette University, M Ed, Education, Teacher Certification
- Ph.D. 1969 University of Wisconsin, Education and Philosophy
- 1983 Post-Doctoral Study-University of Wisconsin, Developmental Reading

Joe himself recalls that one of Sister Nona McGreal's persuasive arguments for him to come to Madison was that he could undertake doctoral studies at the University of Wisconsin. And, with her encouragement, Joe completed his Ph.D.

Joe's interest in a doctoral program did not stop with his own graduation. Through the years, as the Education Department programs developed, his vision and what he terms the Sinsinawa Dominican wisdom in "reading the signs of the times," invited the development of additional programs, teaching licenses, and degrees. As the College grew and expanded, the arrangement of departments gave way to newly organized "schools" in 2005. Among the six schools of the College was now the School of Education, with Dr. Schmiedicke as the inaugural Dean. In 2009, the School of Education boasts programs at the bachelors, masters and doctoral level. Undergraduate programs include at least four majors in Elementary Education, Early Childhood and Special Education, with an additional 15-20 teaching minors and special areas of concentration. Graduate degrees and programs include Master's Degrees and credit areas of Educational Administration, Special Education, Instructional Technology, and General Professional Development. In addition, special programs, conferences and workshops offer much needed professional development credits to teachers.

The crowning glory of this dramatic program growth is the Doctoral Degree (Ed.D) in Educational Leadership. Sam Barosko calls this degree a "lighthouse accomplishment," and recalls that it was at least 12 years in the planning. Professor Bob Reif, who works with the Educational Administration Program, recalls the moment it came to be. "After years of conducting needs assessments, planning, building the foundation, and preparing a most carefully structured proposal, Dr. Joe made the presentation to solicit the Edgewood Faculty Association approval to initiate the Doctor of Education in Educational Leadership Program. After a thorough explanation of the details, and speaking to the objections from some members, Dr. Joe indicated in clear language that "It's Time," and then proceeded to distribute a small battery operated clock (made by daughter Mary Schmiedicke Hong) to each and every member of the Association. I have never seen such a powerful message delivered with a never to be forgotten gift. Needless to say, the Association provided overwhelming approval and support."

Another tribute to the Schmiedicke vision was his support of the Weekend College, remarks Sister Helen Dailey, OP, Director of the Weekend College from 1978-1990. She recalls that he was very involved in getting approval for the graduate programs in education.

Alums recall Dr. Joe as their professor. "I was one of your students in the 1974-1978 era, and I am happy to say that I have had a successful teaching career of 31 years and counting," reminisces Jane Killerlain. Deanna Splitt Freehauf, '66, says, "I have been meaning to write to you the past couple of years to tell you that I LOVED your class and enjoyed your methods of teaching-making class fun, informative and very interesting." Sister Margaret O'Brien, OP, a professor in the Edgewood School of Education for the past 20 years, muses that, "Dr. Joe has been my best buddy in relationship to technological advances in education." Sensing her interest in emerging technology, he invited her to sit in on the course he was teaching: Ed 250: Instructional Resources and Media. Soon Margaret was teaching the course. Then, as she was under pressure to complete a doctorate, Joe handed her a brochure from the California Institute of Integral Studies, an online program. Margaret applied, was accepted, and wrote her doctoral dissertation on *The Integration of Reading and Writing Technology into the Curriculum.*

Margaret Noreuil, Dean of the School of Nursing, captures her thoughts on Joe's contributions to truth. "I always find that I learn something new when I talk with Joe…whether it's about important events in the life of the College, people who have helped us get to where we are today, student experiences over the years, or how we draw on the mission and vision of the College to move forward into the future. I hope that at some point in my life I'm able to offer someone else at least a little of the knowledge I've learned from Joe over the years."

Another example of Dr. Schmiedicke's leading vision and clear insights into the current trends in education was the initiation of the **Edgewood College Education Conference**. Begun in 1991, the conference has attracted the most prominent speakers and researchers in education today, and hosted large groups of local educators, all gathered to improve their own teaching and leadership experience. Attendees at the annual Education Conference were introduced to such notables as Terry Deal, Albert Shanker, Joseph Rezulli, Marian Leibowitz, Art Costa, Bernice McCarthy, and Robert Marzano.

Sister Maggie Hopkins, OP, Director of Mission Integration for Edgewood College, sums up her almost 20 year relationship with Dr. Joe in these words, " What a gift it is for me to count Dr. Joe as my friend, colleague, and collaborator and in so many ways a mentor, these past eighteen plus years at Edgewood. Joe is a man of faith and deep values, with an enthusiasm for life and people.

His approach to just about everything is with integrity, a strong sense of mission, a love of learning and common sense sprinkled with humor. The **teacher/learner** in Joe has been most evident these past few years as he has addressed challenging personal health issues. He shared with me recently that the best way to approach a serious crisis, as he has been, is to 'keep learning as much as you can about it ... and make the doctors laugh.' The 'Dominican' in Joe is reflected in his always 'searching for truth' and his engaging ability to share what he is learning with others."

The serious search for Truth in its many manifestations is continuous and requires a deepening of one's thoughtful reflection, as well as an integration of the other Dominican Values that form the Edgewood tradition. Dr. Joe's life has been defined by this search for truth.

24

COMPASSION

Misericordia

Compassion: Mercy and empathy with another's suffering

- We recognize the intrinsic dignity and interdependence of all creation.
- We acknowledge local issues, sources of injustice and sorrow that make heavy burdens for the people.
- We support and cooperate with each person's efforts to become his/her own best self.

The Dominican Value of Compassion indicates a willingness to respect others and care enough about them to inspire them to become the best persons possible. Professor Cynthia Perry relates an experience that spoke to her and her students of Dr. Joe's compassion. She was teaching a class in Child Life, and her students had many questions about the program for which she didn't have the answers. "Only Dr. Joe knows the answers to your questions," she told her students. She ascertained that he was in his office, so Professor Perry and her students trooped down to the Dean's Office. For the next 45 minutes, they were all crowded in his small office, while he carefully responded to their questions. Cynthia recalls, "The students felt so loved and valued, so important."

A letter, yellowed with age, written in pencil on lined paper, and his response was discovered in Dr. Schmiedicke's files, give evidence of the value of compassion lived out in a most personal way.

Barbara Jordan Elementary

P.O Box 3912

Odessa, Texas 79760

Dear Sir:

I am a third grader at Barbara Jordan Elementary. My class is studying about careers. I would like to be a teacher when I grow up. I would like to know what college courses would help me achieve this goal. Please send me information about your school. I am looking forward to hearing from you. Thank you.

Sincerely,
Nicole Supertzi

Mary Ellen Gevelinger, O.P.

Dr. Schmiedicke's response was filled with a message appropriate to every aspiring teacher:

November 28, 1989

Dear Nicole:

You are very fortunate to be attending a school named after a great teacher. She will be an excellent example to you as you go on in school to prepare for teaching. She learned how to read, write, speak and listen very well. You can also take every opportunity you have to learn about the world around you, about the society in which you live, about the dreams and hopes that people have for themselves and for each other, about people all over the world, and about how we can all work together for a better world.

I hope, Nicole, that you will always hold fast to your desire to be a teacher. We need more teachers to help our young people grow and to help them become the best people that they can be, to make our world a better place in which to live, and to help us all share our planet-earth home.

With this letter, Nicole, I am sending you several booklets and other momentoes (sic) of Edgewood College. I hope that they will help you understand our college a little better and give you the information you need for your school project.

Keep up the good work, and keep your dream alive of becoming a teacher.

Wishing you joy at this time of year and with every personal regard, I am

Sincerely,

Joseph E Schmiedicke, PhD

Chairperson, Department of Education

Undoubtedly, there are numerous tales of a compassionate gesture or response by Dr. Joe, secretly written on the hearts of so many colleagues, students and alums of the College.

25

JUSTICE

Iustitia

Justice: Behavior that recognizes the rights and responsibilities of all God's creation

- We interact with others with integrity.
- We work to assure the rights of all people, especially women and children.
- We commit our energies to issues of poverty and racism.
- We pay just salaries and provide just procedures to hear the concerns of those with whom we minister.

The Edgewood College Value of Justice contains elements of human rights and integrity, along with attention to the eradication of poverty and racism. These elements have been embedded in the curriculum of the teacher preparation program that welcomed young Joe Schmiedicke in the '60's, inviting future teachers to integrate the values into their own lives, and to further them in the lives of their students.

Christine McCarville Hegland, Administrative Assistant to Dr. Schmiedicke since 2000, pays tribute to this value as it related to her life. Although a licensed hairdresser and skilled office manager, she had not completed a college degree. With Dr. Joe's encouragement, and while working full-time, she completed her Bachelor's Degree at Edgewood College in 2008, and proudly marched across the stage at graduation to the cheers of her children and co-workers.

Christine Einerson came to Edgewood College in 2005, to assume a part time position as Administrative Assistant for the Doctoral Program. Dr. Joe, in his usual creative genius, was able to get another part time position approved, and Christine was able to add that position to her own, and thus, become a full time employee of the College. Dr. Joe also added a stipulation to the new position that a Master's Degree was required. This was the encouragement Christine needed to pursue the degree in General Professional Development, and become a proud graduate in December, 2007. "For me, this personal development translated to professional development," Christine reflects.

Another vision and evidence of the value of justice in Dr. Joe's life is the multitude of Professional Development relationships that he has created with so many groups of educators. State laws have always required additional coursework for renewal of the teaching license. Time and cost have been factors that made this difficult for many educators. Through arrangements with Madison Metropolitan School District, many other local school districts, and the Catholic Diocese of Madison, Edgewood College has become known for providing excellent and timely professional development for teachers. These professional development opportunities always carried the opportunity for teachers to receive the credits they required, and at a reduced price. In addition, teachers were exposed to excellent instruction and current research in education. The Edgewood College Education Conference is one example of a professional development opportunity. The John Muir Summer Program for Math, Science and Technology Teachers is another example of longstanding professional development opportunities.

All of these opportunities are designed to send graduates into their profession, prepared to work for a just world through the career of teaching, and to continue their necessary professional development through the years they will teach.

26

COMMUNITY

Communitas

Community: A manner of relating based on our recognition of the interdependence of all nature

- We nurture relationships which enhance the well being of persons, the earth, and all beings.
- We communicate honestly, openly.
- We value cooperation over competition.
- We foster unity in mission that strengthens local leadership and enables the creative, innovative development of gifts for the sake of God's people.

"At the heart of ministry is relationship," a line in the 1990 Constitution of the Dominican Sisters of Sinsinawa,[12] is a description of the way Joe Schmiedicke has approached his work at Edgewood College in the education of young teachers, and his relationship with his colleagues. To those who have known him through the years, Dr. Joe lived these lines before they were set to paper in 1990. He has been diligent in building relationships with faculty, students, alums, and not only building them, but nourishing them. It is assumed that the nourishing also returned to him.

Joe's early days at Edgewood meant that he was surrounded by Dominican Sisters, sisters who became mentors, colleagues and friends, friends to him and to his family. His daughters recall that sisters were present at birthday parties and First Communion celebrations, often bringing a cake to celebrate.

Fr. Tony Schumacher, Chaplain at Edgewood College, remarks that Dr. Joe "Seems to know half the families at Blessed Sacrament Church and has stories about all of them. He is a warm and loving man imbued with the Dominican Spirit."

Graduate Ruth Daly Elderbrook, reminisces that she was a work/study student for Dr. Joe from 1972-1975, and recalls his friendly disposition and smile, and how much she missed him when she graduated. On a visit to campus in 1979, when she walked past Dr. Joe's office he spoke to her and called her by name. "What a remarkable man!"

Breaking bread together has always been at the heart of the Christian tradition of building community. Professor Peter Burke, Director of the Doctoral Program, highlights Dr. Joe's practice of gathering groups around food, of breaking bread together to form community. Breakfasts, lunches, dinners, receptions all have a history around food. Retired Edgewood College President, James Ebben, recalls the annual dinners with student teachers and their cooperating teachers. "Joe would walk from table to table, greeting each cooperating teacher in friendship, honoring them, making them feel so important. It was his way of respecting them." The result was a community of educators, willing to continue the intense activity of preparing new teachers.

Marsha Laundrie, in charge of student practicum placement, echoes the food theme. She laughingly mentions the famous James J. Chocolates, from a local Monroe St. candy shop, that Dr. Joe brings for every occasion, and as often, for no occasion. A recognizable box of the chocolates is like a note left behind, telling that Dr. Joe stopped by.

Dr. Daniel Carey, President of Edgewood College at the writing of this biography, shares a recollection of Dr. Joe's impact on the wider educational community in Wisconsin. "Each year the School of Education at Edgewood College holds a statewide meeting of educators from across Wisconsin – the Annual Education Conference. In the months following my start at Edgewood College, I was invited to attend one of these meetings and to offer a few remarks. What I witnessed during the informal gathering of education professionals was more like a love fest. Dr. Joe Schmiedicke was in his element, surrounded by former students, colleagues and friends carefully gathered over several decades of work at Edgewood College. At that moment, I knew we had a special treasure in the man called Dr. Joe."

Mary Ellen Gevelinger, O.P.

Professors Bob and Ruth Koskela trace their relationship with Dr. Joe back to the 1980's, when they each came to Edgewood College at different times, as adjunct professors. That long history of relationship and support had a high point for the Koskelas when they were both ordained to the diaconate, on the way to Episcopal Priesthood, in Milwaukee. Who should appear in the Congregation but Dr. Joe Schmiedicke! Bob pays tribute to that presence, "You don't understand how much that meant to us."

27

PARTNERSHIP

Consortio

Partnership: A mutual relationship of mature persons who recognize their shared call to actions of justice and love

- We foster unity in mission that strengthens local leadership and enables the creative, innovative development of gifts for the sake of God's people.
- We practice participative decision-making

Partnership, the final Edgewood College Dominican Value, is in itself a *partnership*. Partnerships are collaborative affairs, built on relationships already established, values held in common, visions that are shared, goals arrived at in a community setting.

Many of the stories recounted in discussing the previous values also ultimately point to the partnership that was experience.

Partnerships with the broader educational communities have been a lighthouse in Dr. Joe's circle of influence. Those relationships began early in his life at the college. Joe recalls that he arrived in early July of 1963, but with no classes to teach during the summer, Sister Nona found him a job! During her tenure as President, the Wisconsin Association of Catholic Colleges and Universities (WACCU) was founded, and Sister Nona was an early president of the group. Survey Data were gathered from the 11 member schools by Sister Nona. Young Mr. Schmiedicke was the perfect person to organize and analyze it, and write the report for the WACCU member schools. In the introduction to the report of over 100 pages, in December 1963, he wrote, "In the life of a tree, a seed must be sown before the roots can take hold; the roots must take hold before the tree can grow; and the tree must grow before it can bear fruit." Although written in the context of the emerging WACCU organization, his lines were prophetic of his own emerging career path, reminiscent of the lines from John 2: 20, where the Jews remarked, "This temple has been under construction for 46 years…" [13]

Professor Patrick Fleming reflects on the perception of Edgewood College, and particularly the School of Education, within the Madison Metropolitan School District, across the State of Wisconsin, and beyond. "When I was an elementary and secondary principal, I met Joe at many meetings, CESA gatherings and other events. Joe sat through many *boring* meetings, all the while building credibility for the Edgewood programs, building the foundation for partnerships." Professor Patrick Delmore agrees. "Joe is a person who knows everybody. His extensive contact with persons in the state and local educational community and within the larger Madison community over the past 40 plus years has made him the *face* of Edgewood College."

Sheila Hopkins, TESOL Program Coordinator and Director of the U. S. Office of Education Grant for English Language Learners Programs at Edgewood, attributes Dr. Schmiedicke's vision and support for the successful partnerships with multiple school districts, generated by this grant.

Professor Ellen Browning recalls Joe's encouragement of her ideas for an international partnership. When there were few opportunities for students to have an international experience, she wanted to take students to India to volunteer at a Tibetan Children's Home. Joe was not only supportive, but generous in offering ideas to make the project viable.

Professor Tom Holub recalls an early moment in his time at Edgewood, when he approached Dr. Joe with an idea for taking students to Chicago to work in a partnership in the notorious Cabrini Green Projects. Tom recalls the response from Dr. Schmiedicke, "Do you believe in it?" He never questioned whether there was some hierarchy for permission. Rather, he invited me to search my soul. I appreciated that kind of leadership, and affirmation of my ideas.

Sister Sarah Naughton, OP, Archivist at the College, speaks to Dr. Joe's partnership with the neighborhoods that border the

College. When his family was young, Joe and wife Marian moved to 812 Woodrow Street, just across the street from Edgewood, and in the Dudgeon-Monroe Street Neighborhood. Active herself in the Madison Neighborhood Organizations, Sarah reflects that "through the years he has participated, as a good citizen, in the continuous development of this Central City Neighborhood Association."

Partnership also includes collaborating with professional colleagues. Through the years, Dr. Schmiedicke has been very attuned to the obligation of belonging to professional memberships. A list of these organizations includes membership in at least 20 professional associations. Certificates from many of them offer congratulations on membership for over 25 years.

28

LEADERSHIP

Historia est vitae magistra. **History is the tutor of life.**

The Servant's Reward

One day, when you are in heaven, someone will come up to you
and thank you for the way you touched his or her life.
The person's words will take you completely by surprise.
Soon another person will seek you out, and then another, and
another.

As you listen to each one's story, you will begin to discover all
the ways that God
Used your life when you were unaware of it. You will find that
it was most often

not through the big things you did, but through the small and simple things—

a spoken word that was not planned, a spontaneous act of kindness,

a loving attitude, or a caring smile.

To your joy, you will discover that in all these ways and more,
God used you
to deposit an eternal measure of His love into many needy hearts. —Roy Lessin[14]

dayspring.com

The above poem, offered by alum Deanna (Splitt) Freehauf, '66, in honor of Dr. Joe's retirement, speaks to the aspect of servant leadership that has been a hallmark of his style of leadership. Although not one of the five Edgewood College Values, Leadership is certainly the *secret ingredient* in Dr. Joe Schmiedicke's Recipe for a 46 year Career at the College.

Courtney Moffet, Professor of Special Education, recalls the story of her hiring 16 years ago at the College. Eager to work with this "fabulous person", as she describes him, Courtney worried that the renowned Dr. Schmiedicke might soon leave the College. "How long will you be here?" Dr. Joe responded, "I'm a servant leader. I'll be here as long as you need me." And he has been...a servant to all of us.

Professor Jed Hopkins quotes some Latin, a favorite language of Dr. Joe, in his tribute. "Homo no intelligendo fit omnia."

Dr. Joe: A Lifetime of Service

"Man, in not understanding, makes his world" are the words of 18th century philosopher Giambattista Vico. "Joe, you have truly made your world, and the world of Edgewood, the life of the College not captured by procedural or administrative stuff, but you have managed to keep alive the dimensions of our life that don't get thematised."

Sister Denise Landers, O.P., a Dominican Sister and graduate of the college, recalls her early association with Dr. Joe. "I was at Edgewood when Dr. Schmiedicke first came there as a young man. I was thrilled to see an energetic man with young children who was qualified, competent and committed with us to our educational mission. I was filled with hope and have been delighted that he has given us most of his life's professional energy in leading at Edgewood College. He has successfully directed the school through many phases of development that required a lot of hard work."

Dr. Joe's leadership skills were obviously recognized by the various College Presidents under whom he has served. He was named the Director of Summer School by President Sister Cecilia Carey, O.P., and was instrumental in bringing new programs to campus. National speakers and groups such as Elderhostel were a summer fixture at Edgewood, exposing all participants in the programs to a wider world of truth.

Another title added to Dr. Schmiedicke's impressive list was his appointment to lead the Office of Special Projects, from 1975-1985. Early in this position, he was instrumental in acquiring a grant for the first computer lab at the College. Retired Mathematics

Mary Ellen Gevelinger, O.P.

Professor and former Academic Dean, Sister Marian Harty, O.P., recalls her amazement at his effective, collaborative style. "Dr. Joe would come in and talk with us as a (Math) Department, and then he would go away and write the grant. By listening to us, he knew what we were talking about; we would talk and he would write. We got it the first time we applied for it. It was for hundreds of thousands of dollars, and the purpose was to begin using computers in the math department. The College received a five year grant from the National Science Foundation to create the first Computer Lab. It was about 1977. We trained teachers in computer education."

Another aspect of Dr. Joe's incredible leadership contribution was his participation in the area of NCATE. Membership in the National Council for the Accreditation of Teacher Education is difficult to achieve and maintain, and at the same time very significant to ensure the quality of a teacher education program. Edgewood first received this accreditation in June, 1963, just about the time Dr. Joe arrived at Edgewood. Through the years he became trained as a visiting Team Member for NCATE Accreditation visits to other colleges and universities. His resume notes that he served as the Chair of at least nine NCATE Visiting Teams. He also served as a trainer for team members in another nine states.

With his national recognition as an educational leader and visionary, Dr. Joe served as a consultant to seven or more college and universities across the country through the years.

29

EARLY DAYS AT EDGEWOOD: MENTORS AND FRIENDS

Beatae memoriae **Of Blessed Memory**

News Clippings from Madison newspapers in the 1960's and 1970's, lovingly saved by wife Marian, chronicle the advancement and accomplishments of the young Professor Schmiedicke in his early years at Edgewood College. In the July 15, 1969 issue of The Capital Times, Mr. Joseph Schmiedicke, education, was promoted to associate professor. A year later, in the June 30 edition of the Wisconsin State Journal, he was one of the first four lay faculty members to receive tenure at the college, in the company of colleagues Jewell Fitzgerald, Daniel Guilfoil and Michael Lybarger.

As noted earlier, Joe Schmiedicke was director of the Edgewood Summer Session. A news clipping from the November 5, 1971, edition of the Wisconsin State Journal announced his appointment, effective for the summer of 1972, and noting that he is the "first male faculty ever to head the program." This appointment was effective for many years. Soon after this announcement, on January 31, 1972, The Sheboygan Press announced a $21,095 grant from the National Science Foundation to support a "Cooperative College-School Science Program" during the coming summer.

In the summer of 1973 and in subsequent summers, a series of Liberation Theology Workshops and Bible Workshops were featured in the Summer Sessions, following the closing of the Second Vatican Council, and the increased interest in these topics. Summer Session 1976, according to The Capital Times of June 3, offered courses in reading diagnostics, a music educators' workshop, a History of Religions course for public school teachers, a study of Open Classrooms featuring British educators on campus, organizing learning centers, to name a few.

According to the minutes of the Division of Professional Studies for November 22, 1963, young Mr. Schmiedicke was the sole lay person and the sole male at the meeting, and probably the youngest member of the group. Attendees, according to the minutes in the College Archives, included Sisters Mary Rosary, Melchior, Alexius, Peter Damian, Cajetan, and Mr. Schmiedicke.[15] The same group met on September 10, 1964 with a few changes at the table. Those present were Sisters Mary Rosary, Anthony Daniel, Alexius, Gracia, Mariam, Melchior, and

Mrs. Stevens joined Mr Schmiedicke. He took the minutes for both meetings.

The minutes for these and similar meetings in the next years are significant because they chronicle the emergence of the Department of Education, with Sister Mary Rosary listed as Chairman, in March of 1965. By 1970 there is a memo from Dr. Schmiedicke, Chairman, Teacher Education Committee. Later, on May 4, 1970, a memo also lists him as Chairman of the Department of Education.

Sister Mary Rosary Corrigan was a significant mentor and friend for Joe Schmiedicke during their shared years at the College. Born in 1904 in Chicago, Sister Mary Rosary joined the Edgewood faculty in September of 1941, where she served continuously until June 1, 1975. Her education included degrees from Loyola University in Chicago and Columbia University in New York. With a specialty in early childhood education, Sister Mary Rosary worked with the Department of Public Instruction for the State of Wisconsin to expand the Edgewood K-3 license to become a Nursery School-6 license.

In her book "Edgewood College: A Jubilee History, 1927-1977," Sister Barbara Beyenka, OP details the careful work of Sister Mary Rosary in changing the attitudes of public educators, so that Edgewood student teachers and graduates soon became widely acclaimed and sought after for their outstanding performance. "In recognition of her work the Wisconsin Department of Public Instruction presented her with their distinguished service award when she retired from teaching in 1975."[16] Certainly the young

Schmiedicke watched the work of his supervisor and mentor, and took careful notes.

Joe Schmiedicke's favorite memory of Sister Mary Rosary does not come from the college experience but rather from watching her interact with his daughters, Mary, age 6 and Lisa, age 4. As he tells the story, he noticed that some carpet squares, stored at home, had begun disappearing. When he questioned Mary, she told her dad that Sister Mary Rosary was building a hut in the woods, now recognized as near the site of the Eagle Mound. The carpet squares were for the floor of the hut. About two weeks later, Joe was invited to the hut for a visit. Sister Mary Rosary, in her long white Dominican habit, was sitting in the little hut in the woods, reading *Curious George* to the girls. He recalls that her connection with children in general, and especially with his own children, was remarkable. Even at the time of this writing, there is scarcely a conversation about the early days at Edgewood that does not include the mention of Sister Mary Rosary. Sister Mary Rosary died in 1996, at the age of 91.

Another dear friend and mentor for the young professor was Sister Marie Stephen Reges, O.P., affectionately known to all on campus as "Sister Stevie." Born in 1915 in Washington, D.C., she attended Trinity College, Catholic University of America, Providence College and the University of Wisconsin, and received two honorary doctorates. Sister Stevie arrived at Edgewood College in 1959, and worked and taught in several capacities until her retirement. She began her career as a math teacher, but later moved to the area of Religious Studies, as her passion for

Jewish-Christian Relations evolved. Everyone who knew Sister Stevie believes that her spirit still hovers over the campus. The recording sessions for this biography were all held at a room in the Rennebohm Library overlooking the garden bench, named in memory of Sister Marie Stephen and her friend, Sister Annie Schaudenecker, perhaps in an effort by Dr. Joe to bring Sister Stevie into the conversation. Sister Stevie died May 27, 1997.

Joe shared two reflections on Sister Stevie with Nancy Nelson, as she was assembling a book about her. He has passed them on for inclusion here.

Sister Marie Stephen Reges, O.P. –Woman of Prayer

"My first meeting with Sister Marie Stephen was on the Park and Pleasure Drive along Lake Wingra. Sister Nona McGreal, O.P., President, had assigned me to attend a public lecture at Hillel; Sister Nona had suggested that it might be a good idea to talk with Sister Marie Stephen before I went to the lecture; I asked Sister Mary Rosary Corrigan, O.P., then Chair of the Department of Education, where I might find Sister Marie Stephen. Sister Mary Rosary replied that she was likely saying her "Office" (the prayers of the Divine Office) down on the lake road. The images of "office," "saying," and "lake road" didn't quite compute, but I walked down the lawn in front of Regina Hall, then unfenced, and indeed found a tall solitary figure dressed from head to toe in the former "habit" of the Sisters; she was walking slowly reciting from the book she was carrying. She looked up and greeted me with "My child! What can I do for you? I am Sister Marie Stephen, as she was back then in 1963; "Sister Stevie" would come later. A conversation with a wise and prayerful woman followed."

Sister Marie Stephen Reges, O.P.—Neighbor

"Sister Marie Stephen, by now in 1975, "Sister Stevie" and her companion, Sister Annie Schaudenecker, O.P., lived together in Weber Hall. They had a regular habit of walking through the Woodrow Street neighborhood after their dinner, weather and time permitting. One evening, my youngest daughter, Megan, then five years old, ran into the house and asked what a labor organizer was. 'And what, Megan, brought this up?' 'The Sister Ladies said I will probably grow up to be a labor organizer.' As it turned out, Sister Stevie had noticed Megan lining up about six children from the neighborhood on their bikes for a parade; Stevie was impressed with her organizing skills and thus the comment. As it turns out, Megan, now 36, is an alpha mom; and does indeed keep her three children well organized! The two Sinsinawa Dominican companions patrolling the neighborhood were prescient!!"[17]

Adjunct Professors, Sisters Carol Artery, O.P., and Priscilla Wood, O.P., share their experience of teaching a methods course to aspiring teachers. "When we started teaching in the Education Department in the summer of 1988, little did we know that it also meant the beginning of a wonderful relationship with Dr. Joe. From the first days, his support, encouragement, and belief in what we had to offer made all the difference to us - and that continued for the next 18 years. His visits to our classroom, his attendance at our final programs on the last day, his delight in what was happening made us feel so proud and happy to be part of his department. His knowledge of and obvious love for our Congregation and the Sisters he has worked with over the years always came through in every conversation. We only have wonderful memories of this gentle giant, this brilliant creative thinker, and this caring educator, mentor, and friend."

30

AWARDS, HONORS AND TRIBUTES

Docendo dicitur **It is learned by teaching. Seneca**

Dr. Joe

Late summer fields give
the way he does
opening the Earth so that whoever passes by may freely
partake of the harvest

A very important person waits outside his office
(we have all been Very Important,)
tapping his foot, shifting on the waiting bench while

the Professor
listens to a failing student
(we have all been failures too,)
or listens to a stranger
uncertain about her next steps, alone in a new institution
(we are all strangers once in a while).
Soon the two in the office are laughing,
have shared friends, common memories
and the very important person in the hall
clears his throat and shifts his weight
(we have all been impatient many times).
The Professor does not hurry.

What has he taught us after all?
We leave his office feeling we are more
than when we entered there.
We leave his office feeling that we have been
given a place at the table
of a much larger family,
"i" into "We".

Each of us must move toward this way of Being in the world.
It is not the most efficient way to Be.
Each of us must move toward this way of being in the world.
Everything
depends on this.

Rebecca Zambrano 2009

Mary Ellen Gevelinger, O.P.

The above poem by Rebecca Zambrano, CTELL Project Coordinator in the School of Education, pays tribute to the spirit of welcome and invitation that has been a hallmark of Dr. Joe's style of leadership. That leadership and its influence on the campus has been experienced well beyond the School of Education.

In 1987, the College created the "Stevie Award", named after the beloved Sister Marie Stephen Reges, OP, and given annually to a faculty or staff person who embodies the mission of the college as she did. Dr. Joe was the 6th recipient of this award, in 1992.

The Joseph E. Schmiedicke Future Teacher's Award was created in 2006 by the School of Education. Professor Nancy Nelson was instrumental in establishing this award, and presided at the inaugural ceremony. In her remarks, Nancy explained that the award is "to honor an education student who represents the finest of Edgewood College's Dominican Values. This award is given Dr. Schmiedicke's name because of the dedication of his working life to the promotion of excellence in the preparation of reflective practitioners of education at the undergraduate, post baccalaureate and graduate levels." Criteria for the award include the areas of Dominican values, Scholarship and Leadership, and recipients receive a plaque and a cash gift, from an endowment funded for the Award.

It seems fitting that the final word on Dr. Joe Schmiedicke's contribution to Edgewood should come from a student in the School of Education. Krista Moses was selected to give the undergraduate commencement address at the December, 2008

Dr. Joe: A Lifetime of Service

Commencement Ceremony for Edgewood College, as she received her degree as an Education Major. Krista gave her permission to include selections from her talk in this biography.

"My role is that of the teacher. I am an Education major, and it will become my job to teach, instruct and open the eyes of children on a daily basis. But just as important as math, science, and language arts, are the skills and knowledge to get along peacefully with one another. The study of peace, tolerance, and non-violent conflict resolution will be something that each student in my class will be exposed to daily. I feel it could be the most important thing students can leave my classroom having learned."

These words are taken from an essay I wrote for a philosophy class, and are reflection of the impact of my years at Edgewood College. As soon as I stepped on campus, I could sense that Edgewood was different from other colleges. The campus is a true community where I have felt acceptance, and belonging. The signs adorned with the words Truth. Justice. Community, that hang on light posts around the parking lot are much more than mere decoration. They state and represent the values embodied by people living and working on the campus every day. It was not long before I, too, became a member of this community, and experienced Edgewood's values in a depth I couldn't have anticipated. Each class served to widen my view of the world. From Philosophy, Religion, and English, to my specialized degree-oriented classes in French and Elementary Education, I was taught to think reflectively, critically, and beyond conventional borders. I was encouraged to think in terms of the world community and to examine how my actions would affect the lives of others. Whether that impact was a positive or negative one, would be up to me.

Never was this more apparent than during my Human Issues classes and my Philosophy of Peace class. It was during these courses that I was forced to confront some of the ugliest truths in our world. As the old adage states, "Truth hurts". But what hurts more than any truth… is inaction in the face of an exposed truth. Instructors turned my helpless frustration at the injustices of the world into a passionate desire to serve others and create change in my community. Edgewood made me believe in the power of my own actions and helped to show me that everyone can work small miracles…

All my life, I have thought that I wanted to teach, but at Edgewood, I began to questions this decision. Did I really want to teach? Was that the correct path for me? With such a wide array of engaging classes, I suddenly wasn't sure what to choose as my major. But here, questioning is not simply accepted; it is encouraged. In our classes, we were taught to look at problems and accepted "truths" from all angles and with a critical lens. We were taught to question, examine and reflect on our beliefs and actions. We were able to connect on an intellectual and emotional level that is often lacking in higher education. Teachers cared about our thoughts. And we were eager to learn, from them, and each other. We were encouraged to slow down, think, reflect and question. They are skills we'll always carry with us. And it is because of this deep self-reflection that we now leave Edgewood, feeling more complete as people, and more knowledgeable about our world.

Though my experience at Edgewood has taught me the value of questioning, it has also given me the serenity of secure knowledge. I know, for example, that it has been my courses at Edgewood that have shown me how important my work is. My experiences at the U.N. and Ground zero, powered with the passion of my instructors, brought my own passion for teaching full-circle. When I began student teaching this past semester and I saw the faces of my eager and intelligent students-the faces of our future, everything fell into place. I remember teaching a lesson in which I referenced the country of India. I pulled down the world map to show them where it was located and heard a collective gasp of astonishment behind me. That is what I want to capture for them: the wonder and excitement they get when they are learning about the world. I want them to carry that throughout their lives. Something suddenly clicked inside me. I didn't just want to make the world a better place for my students. I wanted to show them how to change it, and the importance of doing so. To give them the tools, the skills, and the desire to be better than the example we have set for them. I know I have to teach my children in the classroom values I myself have learned at Edgewood. I must teach them to love their community and to work toward its betterment. I must teach them to respect their peers, erasing the hatred and fear that led to the attacks on September 11th. I must teach them that one life can make a difference, that peace is possible, and that we all have an obligation to be a positive force of good in the world. I must teach my students to open their hearts and minds to the opinions and wisdom of others. Most importantly, I will teach my students that it isn't enough to want change; you have to actively live those values each day. Often, community service and justice go hand in hand. But neither of those

Mary Ellen Gevelinger, O.P.

values can be achieved through inaction nor idle hope. We have a duty as community members to serve each other. It was Ghandi who told us, "We have to be the change we wish to see in the world." More than a mantra, this is a life-style embodied by the Edgewood community, and I thank all of you for the positive changes you have created in me. I now hope to one day pass the values I have learned here. I will not simply teach--but serve.[18]

This young teacher with an Edgewood College education, ready to make her mark on the world, epitomizes the effects of Dr. Schmiedicke's 46 year career at Edgewood.

Finis   **A Final Word**

NOTES

1. Personal correspondence of Dr. Joseph Schmiedicke
2. http://www.michigan.gov/documetnts/hal/lm retrieved 2/12/2009
3. http://www.ci.grand-rapids.mi.us/index.pl?page_id=2398 retrieved 2/12/2009
4. http://quickfacts.census.gov/qdf/states/26/2608.html retrieved 11/18/08
5. Paynter,O.P., Mary. *Phoenix From the Fire: A History of Edgewood College.* Madison, Wisconsin. Edgewood College. 2002. 19.
6. Ibid. 31.
7. Ibid. 50.
8. *Relationship: Sinsinawa Dominican Sponsorship.* Sinsinawa, Wisconsin. 9.
9. *Edgewood College Graduate Catalog 2007-2009.* Madison, Wisconsin, 3.
10. Relationship: 9.
11. Recipe courtesy of Dr. Joseph Schmiedicke from family collection.
12. Sinsinawa Dominicans. *Constitution.* Sinsinawa, Wisconsin. 1990. 38.

13. Confraternity of Christian Doctrine, Inc. *New American Bible*. Washington, DC.1970.

14. http:// www.dayspring.com. retrieved 02/05/09.

15. Minutes of the Division of Professional Studies, 11/22/1963. Edgewood College Archives.

16. Beyenka, O.P., Barbara. A Jubilee History: Edgewood College 1927-1957. Madison, Wisconsin, Edgewood College. 1977 44.

17. Personal correspondence of Dr. Joseph Schmiedicke.

18. Moses, Krista. Commencement Speech, December, 2008. Edgewood College. Used by permission of the speaker.

ACKNOWLEDGEMENTS

This biography, a labor of love, could not have been accomplished without the cooperation and shared reflections of so many colleagues and friends. I am grateful to:

-Dr. Joe, for the endless hours of taped interviews, and even more hours of shared stories and collections of family pictures;

-David, Mary, Lisa, and Megan Schmiedicke, for their willingness to retrace the footsteps of childhood, to tell their family story;

-Marsha Callahan and Cherie Schmiedicke, for adding their rich reflections to this story;

Those who agreed to be interviewed: Past Edgewood College presidents:

Sister Nona McGreal, O.P.

Sister Cecilia Carey, O.P.

James Ebben, PhD

Other Colleagues:

Daniel Carey, President

Marian Harty, O.P.

Helen Dailey, O.P.

Margaret O'Brien, O.P

Past and present members of the School of Education, for shared reflections;

Edgewood College Alums who sent reflections and tributes;

Campus colleagues who shared memories;

Doctoral Cohort VII Students;

Lois Hoh, O.P., Sinsinawa Dominican Archivist;

Sarah Naughton, O.P., Edgewood College Archivist;

Ed Taylor and Becky Allen, Communication Office, Edgewood College;

Monica Oboagwina, O.P., Technology;

Christine McCarville Heglund, transcription

Maggie Hopkins, O.P., Office of Mission Integration, Edgewood College

My careful editors: Peter Burke, Sarah Naughton, O.P., Ruth and Robert Koskela, Marilyn Schlosser, O.P., and Bianca Madden, O.P.

And all those colleagues and friends who offered support and encouragement along the way.

Mary Ellen Gevelinger, O.P. March 2009

BIO FOR AUTHOR

Mary Ellen Gevelinger, O.P., EdD, is Director of Doctoral Research at Edgewood College in Madison, Wisconsin. She is a Dominican Sister of Sinsinawa, the founding and sponsoring Order for Edgewood College. As a lifelong educator, she bring her experiences and understanding of classroom teaching and administration to the writing of this biography. Mary Ellen lives in Madison, and happily shares community with her Dominican Sisters, as well as her dog, Dominic.

Printed in the United States
148071LV00004B/2/P